Tolley's Child Care Law Handbook

by
Leo Goodman, *Barrister*
Maggie Rae, *Solicitor*

Tolley Publishing Company Limited
A UNITED NEWSPAPERS PUBLICATION

Published by
Tolley Publishing Company Ltd
Tolley House
2 Addiscombe Road
Croydon
Surrey CR9 5AF England
081-686 9141

Typeset in Great Britain by
Letterpart Ltd, Reigate, Surrey

Printed in Great Britain by
BPCC Wheatons Ltd, Exeter

© Copyright Tolley Publishing Company Ltd 1991
ISBN 0 85459 660-7

Foreword

We have tried to devise a way in which the provisions of the *Children Act 1989* and consequent regulations may be more easily assimilated by all those working with and for children. That is a broad remit covering not only local authority employees but the staff of private and voluntary organisations and lawyers, all of whom will need to be familiar with aspects of both public and private law which are brought together in the Act. As this work is confined to the 1989 Act we have presumed some knowledge of child care law. However, we have included reference to other legislation where appropriate. Parents and community organisations may also find the guide a useful point of reference.

We have not included the Act and regulations in annotated form. Our aim has been to give a ready access to the relevant provisions governing each topic, explain their meaning and significance, and make sufficient reference to the statutory provisions to enable lawyers and social workers to follow up and explore in more detail.

Readers will find a good deal of cross-referencing which, as well as being necessary in an A-Z, is also helpful in appreciating how inter-related the statutory provisions are. Another point of 'style' is that we have dealt with gender by resort to 's/he', 'her/his', rather than accept the rule of interpretation that the masculine includes the feminine. However, occasionally when quoting the Act etc. we have had to accept that rule. Unless otherwise stated references to 'the Act' throughout the text mean the 'Children Act 1989'.

The Act imposes heavy demands on local authorities for both training and a wide variety of resources. The emphasis on consultation and participation will make even more demands on social work time and administrative support, which we have acknowledged. Nevertheless the Act is about 'empowerment', both of local authorities in the services they may or must provide and parents and children in according them a say in decision-making. The Act is very much a statement of the ideal that good practice and adequate resources might achieve, as instanced by the requirements to publicise services and bring them to the attention of those who may be in need of them, and also the 'complaints/representations' procedure which applies to the delivery/non-delivery of services.

The integration of public and private law constitutes a major change which will require new approaches and changes in attitude. This is as true for lawyers as it is for local authorities. We hope this book will contribute to the process.

The authors wish to acknowledge the assistance of Mark Campbell in the preparation of this book.

Maggie Rae
Leo Goodman

Contents

	Page
Stop Press	vi
Table of Statutes	x
Table of Statutory Instruments	xxi
Abbreviations and References	xxv

CHAPTERS

1	Absentees	1
2	Access to Personal Information	2
3	Care and Supervision Orders	3
4	Charges for Services	5
5	Child/Children	7
6	Child Abuse	12
7	Child's Attendance at Court	13
8	Circumcision – Female	14
9	Community Homes	15
10	Complaints and Representations	16
11	Consultation/Participation	22
12	Conduct of Children's Homes	31
13	Contact	35
14	Contributions Towards Maintenance	41
15	Court Structure	43
16	Cross Border Transfer	46
17	Death of Child	48
18	Delay	50
19	Duration of Orders and their Effect	52
20	Emergency Protection of Children	53
21	Family Assistance Orders	68
22	Family Proceedings	69
23	Foster Parents	73
24	Guardians	79
25	Guardians ad litem	81
26	Independent Visitor	85
27	Legal Aid	87
28	Parental Responsibility	89
29	Parties to Proceedings	93
30	Privacy	95
31	Private Fostering	96
32	Race, Religion, Culture and Linguistic Background	100

Contents

		Page
33	Registration and Inspection – Day Care	102
34	Registration and Inspection – Accommodation	110
35	Remands	117
36	Reports to the Court	119
37	Respite Care	120
38	Reviews	121
39	Schools	126
40	Secretary of State's Powers	127
41	Section 8 Orders	128
42	Secure Accommodation	133
43	Self-incrimination	136
44	Support for Families and Children	137
45	Wardship	141
Index		142

Stop Press

Recent legislative changes

The Children (Prescribed Orders – Northern Ireland, Guernsey and Isle of Man) Regulations 1991 (SI 1991 No 2032)

These regulations came into force in October 1991 and provide for certain orders to have effect in Northern Ireland etc. and for certain orders made in the Isle of Man to have effect in England and Wales.

The Children (Secure Accommodation) (No 2) Regulations 1991 (SI 1991 No 2034)

These regulations came into force in October 1991. They make provision for applications under *s* 25 of the *Children Act 1989* for secure accommodation to be made by, and only by, health authorities, NHS trusts, local education authorities, and persons carrying on residential care, nursing or mental nursing homes, in respect of children not looked after by a local authority and accommodated by those agencies or in those homes.

Magistrates' Courts Fees (Amendment) Order 1992 (SI 1992 No 842)

The order came into force on 1 April 1992. New fees in relation to family proceedings are introduced and others significantly increased. The fees are not payable by those receiving legal aid, income support or family credit.

Criminal Justice Act 1991

Part III of the Act deals with children and young persons and deals with children's evidence, responsibilities of parent or guardian, detention pending trial and young offenders. Juvenile courts are renamed Youth courts and their jurisdiction is extended to 17 year olds. In relation to local authorities, they may be ordered to pay the fines etc. of a child who is in their care or provided with accommodation. The court may require a local authority to place a child over 15 in secure accommodation if certain conditions are satisfied. Further, when a child is remanded to local authority accommodation, the court may impose a condition that the child is not placed with a named person. The phasing out of 'unruly' certificates for children of 14 years and over, and the power to remand directly to secure accommodation will be delayed until adequate accommodation is available. The Act will come into force on days appointed by the Secretary of State.

Adoption and the Children Act 1989

A number of adoption agencies have found it difficult to reconcile their practice in relation to children placed for adoption with the placement and review regulations made under the Act. The difficulties arise from the fact that children placed by a local authority for adoption fall within the definition of children 'looked after' by a local authority in *s* 22 of the Act. Further, under *Sch 2, para 15*, the local authority (but not voluntary adoption agencies) has a duty to keep parents informed of the child's whereabouts. Agreements made on placement could, it is suggested, waive the parents rights if it is accepted by all that they should not know the prospective adopters' address.

Stop Press

Miscellaneous

Abduction

The Lord Chancellor's department in conjunction with the Foreign and Commonwealth Office has produced a booklet *Child Abduction*. This outlines procedures available to parents and others with a court order relating to the care of a child if the child is abducted.

Home Office Code of Practice on Video taped Children's Evidence

The advisory code requires professionals using videotapes to keep them secure, but leaves it to professional bodies to issue detailed guidance to members. The code also covers techniques for interviewing suspected victims.

Recent cases

In re B (minors) – Local Government Chronicle – 24 January 1992

On appeal against the refusal to make an interim care order, making instead prohibited steps orders preventing the father from having contact with his children and the mother, and the latter from communicating with the father, it was held that magistrates did not have power to prevent contact between adults. Magistrates were also wrong in not giving the parties an opportunity to address them on the subject of prohibited steps orders as an alternative to interim care orders. Procedure on an appeal is not laid down in the *Family Proceedings Rules 1991* and the appeal was treated as a re-hearing in which evidence could only be called with leave of the court.

Re O – Times Law Report – 6 March 1992

A care order was made because of the child's failure to attend school. The court held magistrates had no power to grant a stay of the order pending appeal. If a stay is required application should be made to the 'stand by' High Court judge.

Re A and Others (Minors) (Wardhsip: child abuse guidelines) 1992 1 All ER 153

This wardship case which was heard in 1990 gives guidance on investigative interviews, drafting of affidavits and disclosure of documents. The revised DOH guidance *Working Together* published in July 1991 reflects changes in practice since the view expressed by Hollings J that 'Disclosure of case conference and similar notes therefore would normally be very much for the decision of the local authority. Application can always be made to the court if a refusal is considered unjustified . . .'. The DOH requires, as a minimum, that written confirmation of the main findings of a case conference, a note of who attended and who was absent, and the recommended plan of action should be sent to parents and other relevant family members who were not present at all or part of the conference. The following guidance is still relevant.

(*a*) Where possible, application should not be made to take children into care *ex parte* and for the initial purpose of a medical examination, unless there is an immediate apprehension of emergency or there are reasonable grounds for believing that the parents would refuse to co-operate in arranging medical examinations.

(*b*) Except in emergencies, case conferences should be held before a child is sought to be removed.

(*c*) Early morning removals of children from their home by police, even though in conjunction with social services, should only be effected when there are clear

Stop Press

grounds for believing significant harm would otherwise be caused to the children or vital evidence is only obtainable by such means.

(d) Good quality video recordings should be the rule.

(e) An overview of disclosure techniques is desirable in complex cases which are likely to be contested. The local authority should consider appointing their own expert at an early stage (if the Official Solicitor is not appointed).

(f) When separate teams work on 'disclosure', social services should appoint an overall co-ordinator to ensure there is no unjustifiable contamination of the disclosures of one team by the disclosures of another team.

Re R (A Minor) [1991] 3 WLR 592 CA

R, a girl of 15, had been admitted to an adolescent psychiatric unit. She suffered periodically from hallucinations and suicidal tendencies; the unit wished to have a free hand to administer anti-psychotic drugs. The local authority commenced wardship proceedings and sought leave for the unit to administer drugs with or without the ward's consent. The case was decided largely on the question of fact – R was held to be not 'Gillick competent' to give or refuse consent to treatment. At the request of the Official Solicitor, the court set out its view on the law generally. The major part of the decision is therefore obiter. The following principles arise from the judgment of Lord Donaldson MR.

(a) No child who might be capable of reaching the standard required by 'Gillick' one day but be sectionable on others could be regarded as Gillick competent.

(b) On reaching competence, the child becomes one more person who can give consent to treatment. The right to consent is not transferred to the child exclusively, nor does the child have a veto on treatment if others consent.

(c) The High Court in wardship has power to disregard the wishes of a Gillick competent minor. This case was cited in *In re J (A Minor) Times Law Report 14 May 1992*. J, aged 16, was anorexic and in the care of the local authority who applied under *s 100(3)* of the 1989 Act for leave to give her medical treatment which she vehemently resisted. It was held that the court had jurisdiction to order that a minor be given medical treatment without her consent. The fact that the child's wishes and feelings were first in the welfare checklist [*CA 89 s 1*], did not give them priority over any other items, including any harm the child had suffered or was at risk of suffering.

The right under *ss 38, 43* and *44* of the 1989 Act to refuse to submit to medical investigation was limited to the stage of assessment.

J v Berkshire County Council CA, Times Law Report 10 March 1992

The President of the Family Division, dismissing the appeal of a mother against a care order, remarked on a case that had been heard by justices over eight consecutive days. When justices are faced with such a lengthy sitting they should consider, he said, whether the case should be transferred to the district registry to be heard by a district judge.

In re P (Minors) Wardship CA, Times Law Report 11 May 1992

The importance of the welfare checklist in *s 1* of the 1989 Act was to remind the court to have regard in particular to the children's wishes and feelings and to make a decision based on the welfare of the child as assessed by the court and not the child. The court should disregard the wishes of children if their welfare appeared to diverge from their expressed wishes.

Stop Press

In re A and W (Minors) (Residence order: leave to apply) CA, Times Law Report 15 May 1992

The child's welfare is not the paramount consideration on an application under *s 10(9)* of the 1989 Act for leave to apply for a residence order pursuant to *s 8*. In granting or refusing an application for leave to apply, the court was not determining a question with regard to the upbringing of the child concerned. As regards residence orders, *s 9(1)* of the Children Act represents a fundamental change to the principle expounded in *A v Liverpool City Council [1982]* AC 791, that a court should not interfere with the local authority's care save in the most exceptional circumstances. *Sections 9(3)* and *10(9)* introduce their own limitations on the persons who might apply for leave, and the circumstances in which they may do so. However, that does not mean that the court gives no weight to the views of the local authority.

Table of Statutes

Access to Health Records Act 1990	2.1
Access to Personal Files Act 1987	2.1, 11.6
Adoption Act 1976	5.3, 11.3, 11.10, 22.3, 22.4
s 6	5.15, 11.10
s 12	5.3, 28.14
s 18	28.14
s 21	15.3
s 26 (repealed)	45.1
Broadcasting Act 1990	30.3
Child Abduction Act 1984	20.1
s 2	20.38
Child Abduction and Custody Act 1985	
s 18	20.38
Child Care Act 1980	5.15, 11.5, 40.2
s 11	26.2
s 18	5.15
s 20	38.2
Part III (repealed)	45.1, 45.3
Child Support Act 1991	22.9
Children Act 1948	32.2
Children Act 1989	2.2, 5.2, 5.4, 5.5, 5.6, 10.2, 10.3, 10.5 10.19, 10.20, 11.3, 11.4, 11.13, 16.2, 16.4, 16.7, 17.6, 19.7, 20.2, 20.12, 20.41, 27.2, 28.2, 28.3, 29.2, 29.4, 30.2, 31.2, 31.9, 34.2, 35.2, 36.2, 37.2, 44.3, 44.7, 45.2, 45.4
s 1	3.2, 20.4, 32.1
(1)	41.2
(3)	3.2, 32.4, 41.2
(3)(a)-(f)	25.4
(3)(a)	5.16
(5)	3.2, 22.6, 41.2
s 2	28.1
(1)	5.3, 28.13
(3)	28.13
(5)	28.12
(7)	28.12
(9)	28.4, 28.12, 44.5, 45.1, 45.4
s 3	28.1
(1)	28.2
(5)	28.12
s 4	28.1, 28.14
(4)	5.8
s 5	24.1
(1)	24.5
(3)	24.4
(4)	24.4

x

Table of Statutes

(5)	24.4
(6)	24.2, 28.14
s 6	24.1
(2)	5.16
s 7	36.1, 36.5, 44.3
s 8	3.4, 5.15, 5.16, 11.27, 13.1, 13.2, 13.4, 13.5, 13.6, 13.8, 15.2, 18.1, 18.3, 19.3, 19.4, 21.2, 22.2, 22.3, 22.5, 28.4, 28.14, 29.3, 29.4, 32.4, 41.1, 41.2, 41.5, 41.6, 41.7, 41.8, 41.10, 41.11, 44.5, 45.2
(1)	41.9
(3)	20.4, 22.1, 22.3
(4)	3.4, 22.3, 22.5
s 9	19.1
(1)	23.1, 45.1
(2)	11.27, 13.4, 41.6, 41.8, 44.5, 45.4
(3)	23.1, 41.8
(5)	11.27, 41.11, 44.5
(6)	19.3, 41.5
(7)	19.3, 41.5
s 10	18.1, 18.3, 22.1
(1)	3.4, 22.2
(4)	41.6
(5)	5.6, 41.6
(7)	29.4
(8)	29.4, 41.7
(9)	41.7
s 11	18.1, 18.2, 18.3, 41.1, 41.2
(3)	41.3
(4)	41.9
(5)	41.9
(7)	13.7, 41.4, 41.5
s 12	41.9
(2)	28.14
s 15	22.9
s 16	21.1
(1)	21.2
(5)	21.2
(6)	21.2
(7)	21.2
s 17	4.2
(1)	37.1, 37.2
(5)	11.22
(8)	4.2
(9)	4.2
(10)	5.7
s 18	4.2, 11.20, 33.1
s 19	11.20
s 20	5.15
(1)	4.6, 23.21
(1)(a),(b),(c)	4.6
(2)	4.7
(3)	4.6
(5)	42.3
(6)	5.16, 11.27
(7)	11.27

Table of Statutes

(8)	11.27, 42.1
(11)	11.27
s 21	4.1, 14.2, 44.5
(1)	4.6
(2)	4.6
(2)(c)(i)	35.3
(3)	4.7
s 22	5.15, 13.1, 20.29, 42.3
(1)(b)	35.2, 37.1, 37.2
(4)	5.16, 11.27, 13.4, 20.29, 35.2, 38.9, 38.10
(5)	5.14, 5.15, 11.24, 11.27, 20.29, 32.4, 38.9
(5)(c)	32.1
s 23	23.1, 35.2
(2)	23.2, 35.2
(2)(a)	23.4
(6)	35.2
(7)	13.3
s 24	10.2, 44.7
(2)	31.3
s 25	29.2, 35.4, 42.1, 42.2, 42.3, 42.7
(6)	42.11
s 26	23.10, 38.1, 38.4
(2)(d)	11.27
(3)	10.1, 10.5, 10.21, 26.6
(7)	10.13, 10.15, 10.16
(7)(b)	10.16
(8)	10.1
s 27	4.1, 11.13, 11.15, 11.17
(1)	4.5
(2)	4.5
(4)	11.15
s 28	11.16
(8)	10.4
s 29	4.1, 4.3
(2)	4.3
(4)	4.4
(7)	4.5, 4.7
(8)	4.5, 4.6, 4.7
(9)	4.5, 4.7, 11.13
s 30(2)	4.7
s 31	27.2, 27.3
(1)	3.3
(1)(b)	19.4
(2)	3.2, 3.4, 3.8
(9)	3.3, 20.6
(10)	20.6, 33.9
s 32	18.1, 18.2, 18.4
s 33(3)	28.14
(6)	32.1
(7)	29.2
s 34	13.1, 13.4, 13.8, 19.6, 29.2, 41.8
(2)	29.4
(3)	10.19
(6)	5.12, 13.4

Table of Statutes

(11)	5.16
s 36	3.9
(3)	3.10
(4)	3.10
(5)	3.10
s 37	3.6, 15.2, 15.3, 20.1, 20.3
s 37(1)	20.5, 29.2
s 38	19.4
(6)	5.8
s 39(1)	29.4
(2)	29.4
(4)	29.2
s 41	20.11, 25.1
(2)	25.4
(3)	5.13
(4)	5.13
(6)	5.13, 25.3, 29.1
s 42	25.1
s 43	13.1, 20.1, 20.4, 20.5, 27.2
(1)	20.5, 20.6
(3)	20.5
(4)	20.5
(5)	20.5
(6)	20.5
(7)	20.5
(8)	5.8, 20.5
(9)	20.5
(10)	20.5
(11)	20.5, 20.7
(12)	20.5
s 44	13.1, 20.1, 20.5, 27.2
(1)	20.5
(1)(a),(b),(c)	20.16
(4)	28.14
(4)(a),(b),(c)	20.5, 20.18
(5)	28.14
(5)(a)	20.18
(5)(b)	20.5, 20.18
(6)	20.5
(7)	5.8, 20.5
(8)	20.5
(9)	20.5
(10)	20.5, 20.20
(11)	20.20
(13)	20.5
(15)	20.5
s 45	20.1, 20.5, 27.2
(7)	20.17
(8)	20.5, 20.22
(10)	20.24
(11)	20.5, 20.23
s 46	13.1, 20.1, 20.5, 20.26
(1)	20.5
(3)	20.5, 20.27

Table of Statutes

(3)(a)	20.5
(3)(c)	20.5
(3)(d)	20.5
(3)(e)	20.27
(3)(f)	4.6
(4)	20.5, 20.27
(6)	20.5, 20.26
(9)	20.28
(10)	20.5
s 47	20.1, 20.3, 20.15
(1)(b)	8.2, 20.5, 20.16
(4)	20.14
(5)	11.18
(6)	20.3, 20.14, 20.16
(9)	11.17
(10)	11.17
(11)	11.17, 20.28
s 48	20.1, 20.30
(1)	20.5, 20.31
(2)	20.31
(3)	20.5, 20.32, 20.33, 20.34
(4)	20.32, 20.34
(5)	20.32
(7)	20.5, 20.25, 20.34
(9)	20.5, 20.33
s 49	20.1, 20.5, 20.37, 20.39
s 50	1.1, 1.4, 20.1, 20.37
(3)	20.5, 20.39, 20.41
s 51	20.1, 20.27
s 53	9.1
(2)(b)	32.1
s 54	9.1
s 55	9.1
s 56	9.1
s 57	9.1
s 58	9.1
s 59(1)(a)	23.4
(4)	10.1
(5)	10.6
s 60	34.2
s 61	10.18, 38.10, 39.1, 39.3
(2)	13.4
(3)	32.4
(3)(c)	32.1
s 62	34.4
(1)	34.4
s 63	23.1, 23.34, 34.3, 39.1
(5)	31.11
(6)	31.11, 34.3, 34.4
s 64	10.18, 13.4, 34.4, 38.10, 39.1
(3)(c)	32.1
(4)	34.4
s 65	34.3
s 66(2)(a)	33.2

Table of Statutes

s 69	31.7
s 70	31.14
s 71	33.1
s 72	33.1, 33.11
s 73	33.1, 33.11
s 74	33.1
(1)(b)	32.1
(2)(b)	32.1
(6)	32.1
s 75	33.1, 33.9
s 76	33.1
s 77	33.1, 33.11, 34.3
(1)	15.3
s 78	33.1
s 79	33.1
s 80	40.1, 40.3
s 81	40.1, 40.4
s 82	40.1, 40.5
s 83	40.1, 40.6
s 84	10.20, 40.2
s 85	34.4
(4)	34.4
s 86	34.4
(3)	34.4
s 87	5.16, 34.4, 39.1, 39.2
(5)	34.4
s 88	5.3, 5.6
s 90(2)	3.7
s 91	19.1
(1)	19.5, 41.8
(2)	19.4, 41.8
(3)	19.4
(4)	19.4, 45.1, 45.4
(5)	19.4
(6)	20.18
(10)	19.3
(11)	19.3
(14)	19.7
(15)	19.8, 20.7
(17)	13.4, 19.6
s 92	15.1
s 93	18.1
s 94	20.5, 20.24
(1)	20.7
s 95	7.1
(4)	7.4
s 97	30.1, 30.2
(5)	30.3
s 98	43.1
s 99	27.1
s 100	45.1, 45.4
(1)	45.1, 45.4
(2)	44.5
(2)(a)	45.4

Table of Statutes

(2)(b)	45.4
(2)(c)	45.4
(2)(d)	45.4
s 101	16.1, 16.7
s 102	15.3, 20.1, 20.5, 20.36
(6)	20.36
s 105	5.2, 5.17, 41.8
(6)	4.7, 34.4
(8)	34.3
Schedule 1	5.2, 22.9, 38.3
Schedule 1, para 16	5.2
Schedule 2	5.7, 12.8, 17.4, 23.1, 38.3, 44.1, 44.4
Schedule 2, para 1	5.7
Schedule 2, para 2	5.7
Schedule 2, para 7	11.19
Schedule 2, para 7(c)	42.1
Schedule 2, para 8	44.5
Schedule 2, para 10(g)	32.1
Schedule 2, para 11	11.24, 11.25, 23.3, 32.1, 32.3
Schedule 2, para 12(e)	32.1
Schedule 2, para 15	11.27, 20.29
Schedule 2, para 16	13.3, 13.4
Schedule 2, para 17	26.1
Schedule 2, para 17(5)(b)	5.8
Schedule 2, para 19	5.8, 15.3
Schedule 2, para 19(1)	29.2
Schedule 2, para 19(2)	23.23
Schedule 2, para 20	17.1, 17.3
Schedule 2, para 22	14.4
Schedule 2, para 23	14.6
Schedule 2, para 25	14.9
Schedule 2, Part III	14.1
Schedule 3	38.3
Schedule 3, para 5	5.8
Schedule 3, para 6(3)	29.2
Schedule 3, para 12	5.8, 5.14
Schedule 3, para 17(1)	29.4
Schedule 3, Part I	20.1, 27.3
Schedule 3, Part II	27.3
Schedule 4	9.1, 12.1, 12.2
Schedule 5	12.1, 12.2
Schedule 6	12.1, 12.2, 34.3
Schedule 6, para 3	34.3
Schedule 6, para 4	34.3
Schedule 6, para 5	34.3
Schedule 6, para 6	34.3
Schedule 6, para 8	34.3
Schedule 6, para 10	10.6
Schedule 6, para 10 (2)(l)	10.1
Schedule 7	23.1, 31.1
Schedule 7, para 2	23.34
Schedule 7, para 3	23.34
Schedule 7, para 4	10.6
Schedule 7, para 6	10.1

Table of Statutes

Schedule 8	31.1, 31.7, 31.8, 31.11
Schedule 8, para 6	31.8
Schedule 8, para 8	15.3, 31.10
Schedule 8, para 9	31.11
Schedule 9	11.20, 33.1, 33.7
Schedule 9, para 2	33.11
Schedule 9, para 8	11.20
Schedule 10, para 3	5.3, 28.14
Schedule 10, para 6	28.14
Schedule 11, para 1(3)	18.1
Schedule 11, para 2	18.1
Schedule 11, para 3(1)	18.1
Schedule 12	45.4
Schedule 12, para 26	35.1
Schedule 12, para 29	35.1, 35.2
Schedule 12, para 33	5.6
Schedule 13	16.6, 45.4
Schedule 13, para 27	5.5
Schedule 13, para 43	5.6
Schedule 13, para 61	5.5
Schedule 14	16.4, 45.2
Schedule 15	45.4
Part I	15.2, 22.3
Part II	15.2, 22.3
Part III	5.5, 10.2, 10.6, 23.10, 41.6, 44.1
Part IV	3.1, 7.2, 15.2, 18.4, 22.3, 32.4, 43.2
Part V	7.2, 14.2, 15.2, 29.2, 43.2, 44.5
Part VI	12.2, 34.1, 34.2
Part VII	12.2, 34.1, 34.2
Part VIII	12.2, 34.1, 34.2
Part IX	31.1
Part X	11.20
Part XI	40.2

Children and Young Persons Act 1933	
s 34	7.5
(1)	7.1
s 39	30.1, 30.3
s 53	14.2, 42.3

Children and Young Persons Act 1969	11.27, 16.2, 16.4, 16.7, 27.3, 32.2, 35.2
s 1	3.8
s 7(7)	27.3
s 12	35.4
s 12AA	1.2
s 16	27.3
(3)	1.2, 27.3
s 23	1.2, 35.1, 35.3, 35.4
(1)	35.3
s 24(5)	26(2)
s 25	16.1, 16.7
s 26	16.1, 16.7

Table of Statutes

s 32	1.1, 20.38
s 70(2)	29.4
Children's Homes Act 1982	12.2, 34.2
Chronically Sick and Disabled Persons Act 1970	5.5
Courts and Legal Services Act 1990	
Schedule 16	16.6
Criminal Law Act 1977	
s 6	20.35
s 7	20.35
s 8	20.35
s 10	20.35
Data Protection Act 1984	2.1, 11.6
Disabled Persons (Services, Consultation and Representation) Act 1986	5.5, 11.3
s 1	11.11
s 2	11.11
s 3	11.11
Domestic Proceedings and Magistrates' Courts Act 1978	5.6, 22.3
s 2	5.6
s 6	5.6
s 7	5.6
s 9 (repealed)	45.1
s 10 (repealed)	45.1
s 88	5.6
Domestic Violence and Matrimonial Proceedings Act 1976	15.2, 22.3
Education Act 1944	
s 37	3.10
Education Act 1981	39.3
s 11(3)(a)	34.2, 34.4
Family Law Reform Act 1969	5.11
s 7(2)	45.1, 45.3, 45.4
s 8(1)	5.11, 28.8
Family Law Reform Act 1987	5.3
Foster Children Act 1980	31.2, 31.9
Guardianship of Minors Act 1973	
s 2 (repealed)	45.1
Interpretation Act 1978	
s 6	41.9
Legal Aid Act 1988	20.1
s 15	27.1
s 15(3C)	27.2
s 15(3D)	27.2
s 15(3E)	27.2
s 19	27.1

Table of Statutes

s 22	27.1, 27.3
Schedule 2, para 2	27.1
Legitimacy Act 1976	5.3
s 1	5.3
s 10	5.3
Local Authority Social Services Act 1970	10.1, 10.5, 37.1, 37.2
s 7	20.28
s 7(1)	10.21
s 7B	10.1, 10.3, 10.21
s 7C	17.4
s 7D	10.1, 10.4, 10.20
Local Government Act 1974	10.1
Part IV	10.1, 10.22
Magistrates' Courts Act 1980	
s 76	20.35
Matrimonial Causes Act 1973	22.3, 22.5
s 41	22.7, 22.8
s 42 (repealed)	45.1
s 52	5.6
Matrimonial Family Proceedings Act 1984	
Part III	22.3
Matrimonial Homes Act 1983	
s 1	22.3
s 9	22.3
Mental Health Act 1983	31.3, 42.3
National Assistance Act 1948	5.5, 5.7, 44.4
s 29	5.5
s 36	10.20
National Health Service Act 1977	
s 22	11.14
Schedule 8	37.1, 37.2
National Health Service and Community Care Act 1990	44.4
Police and Criminal Evidence Act 1984	20.1
s 17(1)	20.35
(1)(e)	20.5
(1), (c), (ii)	20.35
s 38(6)	4.6, 42.8
Prohibition of Female Circumcision Act 1985	8.1
Public Order Act 1936	
s 1	20.35
s 4	20.35
s 5	20.35
Registered Homes Act 1984	12.2, 33.4, 34.2, 34.4, 39.1, 39.3
Registered Homes (Amendment) Act 1991	12.2, 34.1
s 1(4)	34.2

Table of Statutes

Rehabilitation of Offenders Act 1974	26.3
Social Security Act 1986	4.2, 24.2
Social Work Scotland Act 1968	16.5, 16.6
s 72	16.1
s 73	16.1
s 74	16.1
s 75	16.1
Part III	16.4

Table of Statutory Instruments

S.I. No.		
1983/1964	Adoption Agency Regulations 1983	11.10
1989/206	Access to Personal Files (Social Services) Regulations 1989	2.1
1991/975	Inspection of Premises, Children and Records (Independent Schools) Regulations 1991	5.8
1991/890	Arrangements for Placement of Children (General) Regulations 1991	9.1, 11.28, 12.1, 12.13, 13.1, 13.4, 37.1, 37.2, 38.8
	reg 1(3)	38.12
	reg 3	5.16
	reg 4	5.16
	reg 4(3)	38.13
	reg 5	12.17, 13.4
	reg 6	38.15
	reg 7	38.12
	reg 10	38.12, 38.14
	reg 13	37.3
	Sch 1	5.16, 38.15
	Sch 2	38.15
	Sch 3	38.15
	Sch 4	11.28
	Sch 4, para 5(a)	32.1
1991/891	Contact with Children Regulations 1991	5.8, 13.1
	reg 2	5.12, 13.4
	reg 3	13.4
	Sch	13.4
1991/892	Definition of Independent Visitors (Children) Regulations 1991	26.1, 26.2
1991/893	Placement of Children with Parents etc. Regulations 1991	11.28, 23.4
	Sch 1, para 1(h)	32.1
1991/894	Representations Procedure (Children) Regulations 1991	10.1, 35.3
	reg 4	10.9
	reg 5	10.11, 10.14
	reg 6	10.10, 10.11
	reg 7	10.9
	reg 8	10.10
	reg 8(1)	10.13, 10.15
	reg 9(2)	10.15
	reg 10	10.17
1991/895	Review of Children's Cases Regulations 1991	5.15, 9.1, 11.28, 12.1, 12.13, 13.1, 13.4, 38.1
	reg 3	38.7
	reg 7	5.16
	Sch 1	13.4, 38.3
	Sch 3	38.3

Table of Statutory Instruments

1991/910	Foster Placement (Children) Regulations 1991	23.1
	reg 3(3)(b)	23.27
	reg 5(2)(a)	32.1
	reg 5(2)(b)	32.1
	reg 5(6)	23.12, 23.17, 23.25
	reg 8	23.26
	reg 11	23.24
	reg 11(4)	23.24
	reg 12	23.27
	reg 13	23.27
	reg 14(4)	25.5
	reg 15	23.30
	reg 16	23.30
	Sch 1	23.6, 23.7
	Sch 1, para 5	32.1
	Sch 3, para 1(b)	32.1
1991/975	Inspection of Premises, Children and Records (Independent Schools) Regulations 1991	34.4, 40.1
	reg 3(2)	5.8
1991/1247	Family Proceedings Rules 1991	7.1, 18.1, 18.5, 20.1, 30.1, 36.1, 41.1
	r 2.39	22.8
	r 2.40	22.8
	r 4	29.1
	r 4.2	20.7, 25.3, 29.1
	r 4.11	25.4
	r 4.16	30.6
	r 4.16(7)	30.7
	r 4.17	36.3
	r 7	29.1
	r 4.11	20.9
	r 4.14	7.2
1991/1395	Family Proceedings Courts (Children Act 1989) Rules 1991	7.1, 18.1, 18.5, 20.1, 30.1, 36.1, 41.1
	r 2.2	25.3, 29.1
	r 2.3	20.7
	r 2.5	20.15
	r 4.4	8.4
	r 7	29.1
	r 10.7(a)	25.2
	r 11	25.4
	r 11.4	20.9
	r 14.4	7.2
	r 16	30.6
	r 17	36.3
	r 18	20.22
	r 21.7	20.17
	r 21.8	20.15, 20.17
	Sch 2	20.7, 21.17, 29.1
1991/1405	Family Proceedings Courts (Constitution) Rules 1991	15.1, 15.2

Table of Statutory Instruments

1991/1414	Emergency Protection Order (Transfer of Responsibilities) Regulations 1991	20.1, 20.15
1991/1426	Family Proceedings Courts (Constitution) (Metropolitan Area) Rules 1991	15.1, 15.2
1991/1478	Parental Responsibility Agreement Regulations 1991	28.14
1991/1505	Children (Secure Accommodation) Regulations 1991	12.9, 42.1
	reg 4	42.4
	reg 5	42.3
	reg 6	35.4, 42.3
	reg 7	42.3, 42.7, 42.8
	reg 8	42.11
	reg 10	42.9
	reg 14	42.11
	reg 15	11.28, 42.12
	reg 16	11.28, 42.12
	reg 17	11.28
	reg 18	42.2
1991/1506	Children's Homes Regulations 1991	9.1, 12.1, 12.14, 17.6, 34.1, 34.3
	reg 4-14	12.3
	reg 8	12.7
	reg 11	32.1
	reg 16	25.5
	reg 19	12.16
	reg 19(2)(a)	17.1
	reg 23	9.8
	reg 25	34.3
	reg 26	34.3
	reg 28	34.3
	reg 28(2)	34.3
	reg 31(3)	34.4
	reg 32	34.4
	reg 33	34.4
	reg 34	34.4
	Sch 1, para 9	32.1
	Sch 2	12.14
	Sch 2, para 3	32.1
	Sch 2, para 4	32.1
	Sch 3	12.15
1991/1507	Refuges (Children's Homes and Foster Placements) Regulations 1991	20.1, 20.41
1991/1677	Children (Allocation of Proceedings) Order 1991	15.1, 15.2, 15.4, 18.1, 18.6
1991/1689	Childminding and Day Care (Applications for Registration) Regulations 1991	33.1, 33.6
1991/1924	Legal Aid Act 1988 (Children Act 1989) Order 1991	27.1
1991/1925	Legal Aid in Criminal and Care Proceedings (General) (Amendment) No 2 Regulations 1991	27.1
1991/1990	Children Act 1989 (Commencement No 2 -Amendment and Transitional Provisions) Order 1991	45.2

Table of Statutory Instruments

1991/2033	Children (Representations, Placements and Reviews) (Miscellaneous Amendments) Regulations 1991	13.1
1991/2034	Children (Secure Accommodation) (No. 2) Regulations 1991	42.1
1991/2050	Children (Private Arrangements for Fostering) Regulations 1991	31.1
	reg 2	31.6
	reg 2(2)(c)	32.1
	reg 2(2)(m)	5.16
	reg 3	31.11
	reg 4(3)	32.1
	reg 10	31.13
1991/2051	Guardian ad Litem and Reporting Officers (Panels) Regulations 1991	25.1
	reg 4(6)	25.2, 32.1
	reg 7	25.8
	reg 10	25.8
	Sch 1	25.7
	Sch 2	25.7
1991/2076	Childminding and Day Care (Registration and Inspection Fees) Regulations 1991	33.1, 33.6
1991/2094	Disqualification for Caring for Children Regulations 1991	31.1, 33.1, 33.6
1991/2129	Childminding and Day Care (Applications for Registration and Registration and Inspection Fees) (Amendment) Regulations 1991	33.1
1991/2244	Local Authority Social Services (Complaints Procedure) Order 1990	10.1

Abbreviations and References

ABBREVIATIONS – GENERAL

CH	=	Chapter
DOH	=	Department of Health
GAL (RO)	=	Guardian ad Litem (and Reporting Officer)
LA	=	Local Authority
NHS	=	National Health Service
Sch	=	Schedule
SI	=	Statutory Instrument
Reg	=	Regulation
R	=	Rule
Vol	=	Volume

ABBREVIATIONS – STATUTES

CA/The 1989 Act	=	Children Act 1989
CCA	=	Child Care Act 1980
CYPA	=	Children and Young Persons Act 1969
DPMCA	=	Domestic Proceedings and Magistrates Courts Act 1978
FLRA	=	Family Law Reform Acts 1969 and 1987
GMA	=	Guardianship of Minors Acts 1971 and 1973
LASSA	=	Local Authority Social Services Act 1970
MCA	=	Matrimonial Causes Act 1973
MP(M Cts)Act	=	Matrimonial Proceedings (Magistrates' Courts) Act 1960

1 Absentees

1.1 References

Children and Young Persons Act 1969, s 32
Children Act 1989, s 50

1.2 The 1969 Act (as amended) allows a police constable to arrest a child anywhere in the United Kingdom or Channel Islands without a warrant if s/he is absent without consent from:

  (*a*) a place of safety, as a supervised person placed after the issue of a warrant under *CYPA 1969, s 16(3)*;

  (*b*) local authority accommodation as a residential requirement of a supervision order under *CYPA 1969, s 12AA*;

  (*c*) local authority accommodation on remand under *CYPA 1969, s 23*.

1.3 Knowingly compelling, persuading, inviting or assisting a child to be absent is an offence.

1.4 *Section 50* of the *Children Act 1989* provides for the recovery of children who have been unlawfully taken or kept away from local authority care (also those subject to an EPO or in police protection) and also children who have run away or are staying away from care (see RESPITE CARE (37)). A recovery order granted by the court may allow a constable to enter and search specified premises using reasonable force, if necessary. It also operates as a direction to any person in a position to do so to produce the child or disclose information as to the child's whereabouts.

(See also EMERGENCY PROTECTION OF CHILDREN (20).)

2 Access to Personal Information

2.1 **References**

Data Protection Act 1984
Access to Personal Files Act 1987
Access to Health Records Act 1990
Access to Personal Files (Social Services) Regulations 1989 (SI 1989 No 206)
Department of Health (and DHSS) Circulars LAC (87) 10, (88) 16, (88) 17, (89) 2

2.2 The *Children Act 1989* does not modify any of the above legislation. Children are entitled to computerised and other 'accessible personal information' about themselves, if they have the capacity to make an informed request. Parents and others with legal authority to act on behalf of a child, if authorised by the child or acting for one who cannot make an informed request, may also be given access, subject to the right to refuse if it is thought that disclosure would result in serious harm to the physical, mental or emotional health of the child or some other person. (The refusal of health information on the ground of harm to health is limited to harm to the health of the applicant.)

2.3 Reference is made here to the relevant statutory provision and guidance because of the increased and particular emphasis on consultation with and participation by children in decisions affecting them. If children are to be encouraged to express their views they must know the nature of the information held on them, and have confidence that their wishes are adequately recorded.

2.4 The Data Protection Registrar's Guideline (No 5, Revision 1) makes it clear that a child is entitled to request information if s/he understands the nature of the request (the same test applies to non-computerised information). This should be ascertained by interview or, in the case of postal application, a certificate from the parent or other adult, or any other information that the child has sufficient capacity.

2.5 Circular LAC (88) 17 gives guidance on the 'Confidentiality of Personal Information' and the circumstances in which information may be disclosed to other organisations without the individual's consent. The latter, of course, is required by law in some cases, e.g. information to foster parents, GALs, and the disclosure of information e.g. to police in order to prevent or detect serious crime. These principles are not affected by the 1989 Act.

2.6 Guidance for inter-agency co-operation on child abuse is given in *Working Together* (HMSO 1991).

3 Care and Supervision Orders

3.1 References

Part IV of the *Children Act 1989*

3.2 THE GROUNDS

The grounds on which the court can make a care or supervision order are the same and are contained in *s 31(2)* of the Act.

The court will have to be satisfied:

(*a*) that the child concerned is suffering, and is likely to suffer significant harm; and

(*b*) that the harm, or likelihood of harm is attributable to

  (i) the care given to the child, or likely to be given to her/him if the order were not made, not being what it would be reasonable to expect a parent to give to her/him; or

  (ii) the child's being beyond parental control.

The courts must also take into account the provisions of *s 1* of the Act and therefore must

— make the child's welfare the court's paramount consideration;

— consider the welfare check-list set out in *s 1(3)* and take account of the principle set out in *s 1(5)*, that the court should not make an order unless it considers that to do so would be better for the child than not to do so.

3.3 Application for an order

An application for a care order can only be made by a local authority or an authorised person [*CA s 31(1)* and *s 31(9)*]. The only authorised person under the Act is the NSPCC.

3.4 Orders available to the court

The court does not have to make an order even if satisfied that the provisions of *s 31(2)* apply. It may make no order or it can make an order under *s 8* of the Act (see SECTION 8 ORDERS (41) and *s 8(4)*). The court's power to make a *s 8* order is not restricted by an application being made as the court can make the order of its own motion (see *s 10(1)*).

3.5 Jurisdiction

An application for a care or supervision order must be issued in the family proceedings court although it can be transferred to either the care centre or from there to the High Court (see COURT STRUCTURE (15)). The court will probably fix a directions hearing when the application is issued to deal with the timetable for the proceedings, any questions relating to the attendance of the child, the guardian *ad litem's* appointment and investigation of evidence.

3.6 Care and Supervision Orders

3.6 **Interim orders**

The court can make an interim care or supervision order pending the hearing of the final application where in any application for care or supervision orders the proceedings are adjourned or the court has given a direction under *s 37* (see 20.3) and the court is satisfied that there are reasonable grounds for believing that the circumstances as set out in *s 31(2)* of the Act are present in relation to the child.

3.7 **CRIMINAL CARE ORDERS**

Prior to the coming into force of the Act, care orders could be made in criminal proceedings relating to juveniles. The court's power to make such orders has been abolished by *s 90(2)* of the Act. Criminal care orders in force on 14 October 1991 ceased to have effect on 13 April 1992.

3.8 **Education supervision orders**

Prior to the Act coming into force, it was possible for a care order to be made on the grounds that a child was of compulsory school age and was not receiving sufficient full-time education suitable to her/his age, ability, aptitude and any special education needs that the child might have [see *CYPA 1969, s 1*]. That power has now been removed and it is not possible to make a care order on the basis of a child not being properly educated. A care order can now be made only if the grounds set out in *s 31(2)* of the Act are met and it can only be made on the application of the local authority or the NSPCC.

3.9 A local education authority can, however, apply for an education supervision order [see *s 36*]. The application should be made to the family proceedings court but can in certain circumstances be transferred to another court.

A court can only make an education supervision order if the following requirements are met:

— the child is of compulsory school age; and

— the child is not being properly educated.

3.10 'Properly educated' is defined as receiving efficient full-time education suitable to the child's age, ability and aptitude and any special educational needs the child may have [*s 36(3)* and *(4)*]. The court can deem the child is not being properly educated if the child is the subject of a school attendance order under *s 37* of the *Education Act 1944* which has not been complied with or is a registered pupil at a school which s/he is not attending regularly [*s 36(5)*].

4 Charges for Services

4.1 References
Children Act 1989, ss 21, 27 and *29*

4.2 INDIVIDUAL LIABILITY
Local authorities are able to charge for services (other than advice, guidance and counselling) provided under their general duty to safeguard and promote the welfare of children in need and promote the upbringing of such children by their families [*CA ss 17* and *18*]. Such services include day care for children under five not attending school whether or not in need, and care or supervised activities for children attending school out of school hours or during school holidays.

The services will include assistance in kind, or, in exceptional circumstances, cash. In that case, where the service is conditional on repayment in whole or in part, the local authority must, before giving the assistance or imposing conditions as to repayment, consider the means of the child and each of her/his parents. No-one while in receipt of income support or family credit will be liable to make any such repayment [*CA s 17(8)* and *(9)*]. Repayment may be demanded at any time – for example, if the parent comes off income support. That is the interpretation given to the wording of *s 17(9)* 'No person shall be liable to make any repayment of assistance or its value at any time when he is in receipt of income support or family credit under the Social Security Act 1986'.

4.3 Services such as attendance at day care, family centres, holidays and home helps can be subject to charges which the local authority consider reasonable. Presumably the recovery of the full cost of a service would be a reasonable basis of charging subject to any abatement (see 4.4 below). The authority are not bound to charge; the Act is permissive in this respect [*CA s 29*]. However, if a charge is levied no person can be required to pay more than can be reasonably expected of her/him if the authority is satisfied her/his means are sufficient for it to be reasonably practicable for her/him to pay the charge [*CA s 29(2)*].

4.4 Some form of means testing will inevitably be required and flat-rate charges will be ruled out. No-one is liable to pay a charge at any time when they are in receipt of income support or family credit.

Various methods of assessing ability to pay could be used – disposable income with a sliding scale of charges from the maximum related to the true cost of the service, for example. Local authorities have total discretion whether to charge or not and to give discretion to exempt or abate charges. The persons liable to be charged for services provided are:

(*a*) each of the child's parents where the service is provided for a child over 16;

(*b*) the child her/himself where the service is provided for a child over 16; and

(*c*) members of a child's family where the service is provided for that person [*CA s 29(4)*].

4.5 Charges for Services

4.5 INTER-AUTHORITY CHARGES

Local authorities will from time to time accommodate children who are or were ordinarily resident in the area of another authority. In such cases the Act provides for the recovery of any reasonable expenses incurred in providing accommodation and maintaining the child [CA s 29(7) and (8)].

When a local authority gives assistance in response to a request from another local authority, they may recover any expenses reasonably incurred from that authority [CA ss 27(1), (2) and 29(9)].

4.6 The circumstances in which one authority will accommodate or maintain a child ordinarily resident in another authority's area are as follows.

   (*a*) Where a child is found to be in need, for example, s/he has been lost or abandoned, the authority for the area where the child is found have the statutory duties in relation to the child and her/his family. If accommodation is provided the cost of that is recoverable from the authority where s/he is ordinarily resident. Costs of accommodation and maintenance do not include costs of social work time or any administrative expenses. The child's home authority should be notified in writing when accommodation is provided and that authority may within three months (or longer if such a period is prescribed by regulations) 'take over' the provision of accommodation. In effect they may transfer the child so that they will be 'looking after' her/him in any way they are able. It would seem that when a child over 16 is found to be in need other than as a result of the three circumstances set out in *s 20(1)(a), (b)* and *(c)*, for example, a child over 16 requests accommodation and is accepted because her/his welfare would otherwise be seriously prejudiced, the cost of accommodation cannot be recovered from the 'home' authority. The provision for recovery of costs is specifically related to the circumstances in *s 20(1)* and therefore does not cover accommodation under *s 20(3)*.

   (*b*) Where accommodation is provided other than in their own community home or a controlled home or hospital vested in the Secretary of State by reason of:

   (i) a child assessment or emergency protection order,

   (ii) a request to receive from police protection under *s 46(3)(f)* (see 20.26 below), or

   (iii) a request to receive under *s 38(6) Police and Criminal Evidence Act 1984* (arrangements for a juvenile in custody to be removed to LA accommodation and detained there) [CA ss 21(1), (2) and 29(8)].

4.7 Ordinary residence

In determining 'ordinary residence', periods in which a child lives in a school or other institution or any place in accordance with the requirements of a supervision order or while accommodated by or on behalf of a local authority, are disregarded [*s 105(6)*]. Any question under *s 20(2), 21(3)* or *29(7)-(9)* as to the ordinary residence of a child shall be determined by agreement between the local authorities, or in default of agreement by the Secretary of State [CA s 30(2)].

5 Child/Children

5.1 References

See text below at 5.8.

5.2 DEFINITIONS

Definition of child

'Child' in the *Children Act 1989* means a person under the age of 18 [*CA s 105*]. A person attains a given age at midnight of the day proceeding the anniversary of her/his birth. The one exception to this definition in the 1989 Act is in *Schedule 1* 'financial provision for children' which provides, *inter alia*, for the extension of payments beyond the age of 18 in certain circumstances [*Sch 1 para 16*].

5.3 Legitimate children – The Family Law Reform Act 1987

The legal disabilities attaching to illegitimacy have now virtually disappeared and the principle now is that the position of a child born to unmarried parents should be the same as that of one born to married parents. References to any relationship between two persons are to be construed without regard to whether the father or mother have or had been married to each other at any time. This rule applies to all legislation passed, and legal documents drawn up, after the *Family Law Reform Act 1987* came into force on 4 April 1988. The 1987 Act further provides that from the above date, references to a person whose father and mother were married to each other at the time of her/his birth include a child legitimated by *ss 1* or *10* of the *Legitimacy Act 1976*, an adopted child, or a child otherwise treated in law as legitimate. Conversely, references to a person whose father and mother were not married at the time of her/his birth do not include any of the above category of children.

In determining parental responsibility, therefore, under the *Children Act 1989, s 2(1)* (which deals with a child's mother and father being married to each other at the time of her/his birth) these words are taken to include adoptive parents although the *Adoption Act 1976* itself gives parental responsibility to the adoptive parents [*Adoption Act 1976, s 12* as amended by *CA s 88* and *Sch 10, para 3*].

5.4

It is important to remember that this definition of child is for the purposes of the *Children Act* and may be modified or qualified in other legislation. Indeed, a person who has reached the age of 17, or 16 if married, though still a child while under the age of 18 may not be made the subject of a care or supervision order under the 1989 Act [*CA s 31(3)*].

5.5 Disabled children

Consistency has been achieved in relation to disabled children so that in the *Disabled Persons (Services, Consultation and Representation) Act 1986*, 'disabled person' now means, in the case of a person under the age of 18, a person

5.6 Child/Children

who is disabled within the meaning of *Part III* of the *Children Act 1989* [*CA Sch 13 para 61*].

Similarly the *Chronically Sick and Disabled Persons Act 1970* applies with respect to disabled children as defined by the *Children Act 1989* in relation to whom the local authority have functions under *Part III* of the Act, as it applies to persons to whom *s 29 of the National Assistance Act 1948* applies [*Sch 13 para 27*].

These amendments are necessary because in bringing disabled children within the definition of 'children in need' in the 1989 Act, the *National Assistance Act 1948* now applies to persons aged 18 and over. The effect is that local authorities have duties to provide support under *Part III* of the 1989 Act for disabled children, as for all other children in need.

5.6 Child of the family

Where a court is considering making a decree of divorce, annulment or separation affecting children of the family, consideration must be given in the light of arrangements made or proposed by the court as to whether it should exercise any of its powers under the *Children Act 1989*. The court is also given power to hold off making the decree absolute until further order if it is likely to be required to exercise those powers but is not yet in a position to do so.

(The definition of 'child of the family' in *s 52* of the *Matrimonial Causes Act 1973* is as amended by *Sch 12, para 33* of the 1989 Act.)

Under the *Domestic Proceedings and Magistrates' Courts Act 1978*, the court cannot dismiss or make a final order on an application under *ss 2, 6* or *7* where there is a child of the family, unless it has decided whether or not to exercise any of its powers under the *Children Act* with respect to the child. 'Child of the family' is defined in *s 88* of the 1978 Act as amended by *Sch 13, para 43* of the 1989 Act. Any party to a marriage, whether subsisting or not, is entitled to apply for a residence or contact order with respect to a child who is a child of the family [*CA 1989, s 10(5)*].

5.7 Child in need – s 17(10)

The Act defines 'in need' in broad terms including 'disability' which is defined much as for adults under the *National Assistance Act 1948*. The local authority has a duty to provide services for children in need to safeguard and promote welfare and to promote upbringing of children by their families. 'Family' for this purpose includes any person who has parental responsibility for the child and any other person with whom s/he has been living. The local authority then has to provide a wide range of services directly or through her/his family designed to enable a child to achieve a reasonable standard of health and development, to avoid significant impairment of health and development, and to cope with particular disability. Health means physical or mental health and development means physical, intellectual, emotional, social and behavioural development. A child's needs will be related to age, sex, race, religion, culture and language and therefore these features of the services are emphasised in *Schedule 2* which deals in detail with services for children in need (see SUPPORT FOR FAMILIES AND CHILDREN (44)) [*CA Sch 2, paras 1* and *2*].

5.8 CHILD OF SUFFICIENT UNDERSTANDING

Children Act 1989, ss 4(4), 38(6), 43(8), 44(7), Sch 2, paras 17(5)(b) and *19* and *Sch 3, paras 5* and *12*

Inspection of Premises, Children and Records (Independent Schools) Regulations 1991 (SI 1991 No 975), reg 3(2)
Contact with Children Regulations 1991 (SI 1991 No 891)

5.9 The courts are given powers to direct examinations and assessments when making interim care, child assessment, and emergency protection and supervision orders. Similarly, a child in an independent school, for example, may be examined on an inspection. Nevertheless, a child of sufficient understanding to make an informed decision may refuse to submit to the examination or assessment. With the leave of the court a child of sufficient understanding may apply for the revocation of a parental responsibility agreement. The Act does not attempt a definition of 'sufficient understanding'. These provisions are an important statement of children's rights reflecting the judgment in the House of Lords in *Gillick v West Norfolk Health Authority* (*1985 3 All ER, p 402*) which decided that a child (although under 16) of sufficient understanding and intelligence to understand what is proposed, has the right to make her/his own decisions. Therefore, neither the rights, duties, powers and responsibilities attaching in law to parental responsibility, nor the court's powers in the instances cited will override the decisions of a child of sufficient understanding. Whether a child has reached that point is a question of fact and no doubt will be judged by the court on the advice of adults, for example, a guardian *ad litem* who has specific duties in that regard. The child will need information to be able to come to an informed decision and social workers and guardians may be expected to make the relevant information available.

5.10 **Medical advice and treatment**

In relation to contraceptive advice and treatment, the House of Lords decided in *Gillick* that doctors should always seek to persuade a child to agree to the parents being informed. However, where the child refuses either to tell parents or permit the doctor to do so, the doctor will be justified in proceeding without the parents consent or even knowledge provided that s/he is satisfied

(*a*) that the girl, although under 16 years of age will understand the doctor's advice;

(*b*) that the doctor cannot persuade the girl to inform her parents or allow her/him to inform her parents that she is seeking contraceptive advice;

(*c*) that she is likely to begin or continue having sexual intercourse with or without contraceptive treatment;

(*d*) that unless she receives contraceptive advice or treatment her physical and mental health or both are likely to suffer; and

(*e*) that her best interest requires him to give her contraceptive advice, treatment or both without parental consent.

This proposition by one Lord Justice of Appeal appears more constraining than the judgment of Lord Scarman who said 'it would be a question of fact whether a child seeking advice has sufficient understanding of what is involved to give a consent in law. Until the child achieves the capacity to consent the parental right to make the decision continues save only in exceptional circumstances'. The first proposition was incorporated in DHSS Circular LAC (86)3 giving guidance to health authorities and others.

5.11 For children of 16 and over, their consent to any surgical, medical or dental treatment is as effective as if they were of full age, and where such consent has

5.12 Child/Children

been given it is not necessary to obtain any consent from the parent or guardian [*Family Law Reform Act 1969, s 8(1)*].

5.12 A child of sufficient understanding may be granted leave to apply for a *s 8* order. The child may also refuse or cancel the appointment of an independent visitor. The consent of a child in care to arrangements to live abroad is required unless s/he is not of sufficient understanding. Refusal of contact under the *Children Act 1989, s 34(6)* must be notified to a child of sufficient understanding [*SI 1991 No 891, reg 2*].

5.13 **Child's understanding and legal representation** – *s 41(3) and (4)*

The court in specified proceedings [*CA s 41(6)*] may appoint a solicitor to represent a child if no guardian *ad litem* has been appointed and it is in the child's best interests, if the child has sufficient understanding to instruct a solicitor and wishes to do so. Where a guardian has been appointed s/he may instruct a solicitor for the child in accordance with the rules. However, the solicitor must take instructions from a child of sufficient understanding who wishes to give instructions which are in conflict with those of the guardian.

5.14 **Child's age and understanding**

Education supervision orders – *Sch 3, para 12*

The supervisor under an education supervision order may give directions to the child to ensure that s/he is properly educated. Before imposing the directions the supervisor must ascertain the child's wishes and feelings and shall give due consideration, having regard to the child's age and understanding, to such wishes and feelings. The introduction of the word 'age' departs from the formulation adopted for medical and other assessments but is the same as under the general duty of a local authority with regard to children they are looking after or proposing to look after [*CA s 22(5)*]. Understanding is not necessarily related to chronological age. The phrase would seem to permit the wishes of a young child with sufficient understanding to be disregarded, or conversely, the wishes of an older child with limited understanding to be followed. It would be more sensible to give the consideration due to a child's understanding. Somewhat perversely, a guardian's duty is to give such advice to a child as is appropriate 'having regard to her/his understanding'.

5.15 **Decisions in relation to children**

It would seem that the wording of the *Child Care Act 1980, s 18* and the *Adoption Act 1976, s 6* have in effect been re-enacted in *ss 20* and *22(5)*: 'give due consideration having regard to the child's age and understanding'. This joining of age with understanding was construed in a Court of Appeal case concerning the adoption of two girls aged thirteen and ten and a half (*In re D (Minors) 1981 21 Family Law Reports 102*).

> 'The court is required to ascertain as far as practicable the wishes and feelings of the child regarding the decision and give due consideration to them. That to my mind must be an important consideration when dealing with children of the age of these children. They are fully old enough to understand the broad implications of adoption ... if they actively wish to be adopted even if they cannot give a very coherent reason for that wish ... to refuse an adoption in the face of that wish does require ... some fairly clear reason'.

That interpretation is applicable to *ss 20* and *22*, although the coupling of age with understanding may be thought to be unfortunate.

In proceedings relating to an opposed *s 8* order or care and supervision proceedings, courts must have regard (but not give due consideration) to the ascertainable wishes and feelings of the child concerned, considered in the light of her/his age and understanding. Various other provisions of the Act allow a child of any age to make applications, for example, for granting or refusing contact while under a care order. Children making such applications will need the help of adults in explaining entitlements and indeed the *Review of Children's Cases Regulations 1991 (SI 1991 No 895)* place a duty on the local authority to inform the child so far as reasonably practical of any step s/he may take under the Act.

5.16 CHILD'S VIEWS, WISHES AND FEELINGS

A child's wishes and feelings must be ascertained and regard had or due consideration given to them in a variety of circumstances set out in the Act, many of which are re-enacted from previous legislation. Social workers will necessarily be involved in identifying and reporting on them.

Courts hearing applications relating to *s 8* orders, or care and supervision order proceedings must have regard to ascertainable wishes and feelings of the child concerned [*CA s 1(3)(a)*]. Before providing accommodation for a child a local authority must, so far as is reasonably practical and consistent with a child's welfare, ascertain his wishes and give due consideration to them [*CA s 20(6)*]. Before making any decision about a child subject to a care order or accommodated by a local authority or who it is proposed should be in care or accommodated (looked after), a local authority must, so far as is reasonably practicable, ascertain his wishes and feelings and give due consideration to them [*CA s 22(4)*]. Before conducting any review the local authority must, unless it is not practicable to do so, seek and take into account the views of the child [*reg 7, SI 1991 No 895*]. Before making a care order the court must invite the parties to the proceedings, and this includes the child, to comment on the proposed arrangements for contact [*CA s 34(11)*]. Local authorities must make immediate and long-term arrangements, so far as practicable, before any placement of a child and in doing so must consider her/his wishes and feelings having regard to her/his age and understanding [*regs 3* and *4* and *Sch 1* of *Arrangements for Placement of Children (General) Regulations 1991 (SI 1991 No 890)*]. The wishes and feelings of a privately fostered child regarding the arrangements should be ascertained when the local authority visits to satisfy itself as to the child's welfare [*CA s 67* and the *Children (Private Arrangements for Fostering) Regulations 1991 (SI 1991 No 2050), reg 2(2)(m)*].

(See also CONSULTATION/PARTICIPATION (11).)

5.17 CHILD-UPBRINGING

Upbringing includes the care of a child but not her/his maintenance [*CA s 105*].

6 Child Abuse

6.1 **References**

Working Together (HMSO 1991)

6.2 The *Children Act 1989* provides a new framework for the care and protection of children. Courts have new powers and duties and parents etc. are now more involved in decision-making. The changes are dealt with under separate headings elsewhere. The guidance, issued by the Home Office, DOH, Welsh Office and DES, *Working Together* has been revised to take account of the Act and other recent developments, including reports of inquiries into child abuse.

6.3 The guidance requires separate study along with associated material for professional staff involved in assessment and investigation etc.

6.4 Some points which are new or receive increased emphasis are the consideration of 'pre-birth' case conferences and the attendance of parents, carers and children at case conferences (they should attend unless good reason to exclude can be shown, in which case this must be recorded in the minutes).

6.5 The timing of intervention or removal of children from home in cases of organised abuse is touched on, but further guidance on 'organised abuse' must await the completion of a research study commissioned by the DOH.

6.6 A child abuse investigation should be considered if it is thought that a child is likely to suffer significant harm as a result of female circumcision (see CIRCUMCISION – FEMALE (8)).

7 Child's Attendance at Court

7.1 **References**

Children Act 1989, s 95
Children and Young Persons Act 1933, s 34(1)
Family Proceedings Courts (Children Act 1989) Rules 1991 (SI 1991 No 1395)
Family Proceedings Rules 1991 (SI 1991 No 1247)

7.2 A child of any age concerned in proceedings under *Parts IV* and *V* of the Act (care and supervision/protection of children) may be ordered to attend court at any stage of the hearing. Under the rules the court must consider whether to give directions for attendance [*SI 1991 No 1395, r 14(4)* and *SI 1991 No 1247, r 4(14)*].

7.3 The court may also order any person, in a position to do so, to disclose information about the whereabouts of the child or bring her/him to court.

7.4 If there is reason to believe that an order to attend will not or has not been complied with, the court may authorise a police constable to bring the child to court and to enter and search specified premises if there is reasonable cause to believe the child may be found there [*CA s 95(4)*].

7.5 Where a child is brought before a court for any reason, any parent or guardian may be required to attend and must be so required at any stage where the court thinks it desirable unless it would be unreasonable to require attendance [*CYPA 1933, s 34*].

8 Circumcision – Female

8.1 **References**

Prohibition of Female Circumcision Act 1985
Working Together (HMSO 1991)

8.2 Local authorities have a duty to investigate where they have reasonable grounds to suspect that a child is likely to suffer significant harm and consider what action is necessary to safeguard the child's welfare [*CA s 47(1)(b)*].

8.3 A child abuse investigation should be considered by the local authority if it is thought a child is likely to suffer significant harm as a result of female circumcision (see *Working Together* p 11).

8.4 A care, prohibited steps or other order may be appropriate in order to prevent actions likely to cause significant harm. An application for a prohibited steps or emergency protection order may be made *ex parte* to a family proceedings court with the leave of the justices' clerk [*Family Proceedings Courts (Children Act 1989) Rules r 4(4)*].

9 Community Homes

9.1 **References**

Children Act 1989, ss 53–58 and *Sch 4*
Children's Homes Regulations 1991 (SI 1991 No 1506)
Arrangements for Placement of Children (General) Regulations 1991 (SI 1991 No 890)
Review of Children's Cases Regulations 1991 (SI 1991 No 895)

9.2 Each local authority itself, or in conjunction with others, is responsible for providing children's homes suitable for the various needs of children. Such 'community' homes may be directly maintained by a local authority or provided by a voluntary organisation. If the home is provided by a voluntary organisation, but the management, equipment and maintenance of the home is to be a local authority responsibility, it is a controlled community home. If otherwise, it is an assisted community home.

9.3 The Secretary of State has powers to stop the use of a home which is unsatisfactory and determine disputes between local authorities and the voluntary organisation providing a controlled or assisted home.

9.4 Once a controlled or assisted home is established, two years notice of cessation is required either by the voluntary organisation or the local authority. Provision is made for financial compensation on cessation related to the value of the premises, attributable to the expenditure incurred in relation to the premises by the Secretary of State or the local authority.

9.5 Instruments of management, made by the Secretary of State for controlled and assisted homes will provide for a body of managers, two-thirds of whom will be appointed by the local authority responsible for a controlled home and one-third in the case of an assisted home.

9.6 The management, equipment and maintenance of an assisted home is the responsibility of the voluntary organisation and the local authority is responsible for a controlled home. The functions of both homes are exercised through the body of managers. The instrument of management may reserve matters to the authority/voluntary organisation, and notice may be given to reserve any matter. However, employment of staff at a community home is always the responsibility of the local authority for a controlled home and the voluntary organisation for an assisted home. In a controlled home the authority may allow the voluntary organisation, e.g. a religious order, to employ persons for duties in the home.

9.7 Any proposal to employ or terminate employment by a voluntary organisation must be notified to the local authority who may refuse consent. The local authority itself may, after consultation with the voluntary organisation, require them to terminate an employment.

9.8 The Secretary of State is empowered by *reg 23, SI 1991 No 1506* to give and revoke directions to any community home to accommodate a child looked after by a local authority for whom no places are normally available or take such action in relation to a child as may be specified.

10 Complaints and Representations

10.1 **References**

Children Act 1989, ss 26(3), (8), 59(4) and *Sch 6, para 10 (2)(1), Sch 7, para 6*
Representations Procedure (Children) Regulations 1991 (SI 1991 No 894)
Department of Health guidance Vol 4 Ch 5, Vol 3 Ch 10
Local Authority Social Services Act 1970, ss 7B and *7D*
Local Authority Social Services (Complaints Procedure) Order 1990 (SI 1990 No 2244)
Local Government Act 1974, Part IV

10.2 **APPLICATION PROCEDURE**

The procedure for dealing with any representations (including any complaint) which the *Children Act* and regulations have established applies to 'the discharge by the authority of any of their functions under *Part III* of the Act in relation to the child'. It applies to children being looked after by a local authority, or who are in need, and also to those qualifying for advice and assistance under *s 24* and by virtue of the regulation-making powers in the Act to both registered and voluntary children's homes and exemptions to the 'usual fostering limit'. It is designed to cover all representations regarding a local authority's actions in relation to any child in need or looked after by a local authority and representations made to a voluntary organisation or registered children's home providing accommodation for a child who is not being looked after by a local authority.

10.3 Representations and complaints about other child care matters may be covered by the Complaints Procedure Directions issued under the *Local Authority Social Services Act 1970, s 7B*, and it is suggested in DOH guidance that even non-statutory functions such as the inclusion of a child's name on a child protection register could be dealt with under these or analogous procedures. Both procedures will create common structures, although that under the *Children Act* requires the involvement of an independent person at each stage of the procedure.

10.4 It should be noted that other avenues of complaint will still be open, e.g. reference to the ombudsman or elected local authority members, and, under *s 7D* of the *Local Authority Social Services Act 1970*, default powers of the Secretary of State. *Section 26(8)* requires the local authority to give such publicity as considered appropriate to the procedures under the Act.

10.5 **Grounds for representations**

Section 26(3) does not define representations. The DOH guidance defines representations as including 'enquiries and statements about such matters as the availability, delivery and nature of services and will not necessarily be critical'. The guidance defines 'complaint' as 'a written or oral expression of dissatisfaction or disquiet in relation to an individual child either as a result of an unwelcome or disputed decision, concern about the quality or appropriateness of services, delay in decision making about services or about their delivery or non-delivery . . .'. For convenience the term complaint is used in this section to include representations.

Complaints and Representations 10.7

There can be little doubt that there is now a most wide-reaching scheme for complaints regarding the nature, quality or delivery of any local authority personal social services function (including disabled children who may also come specifically under the complaints procedure for community care services). Publicity must be given as considered appropriate to schemes under the 1989 and 1970 Acts. It would be advisable to see that all users or prospective users of the personal social services receive, or have available, relevant information (see detailed guidance given by DOH).

10.6 **The complainant**

Representations may be received from:

— any child being looked after by a local authority or who is in need;

— any child (not so being looked after) provided with accommodation by a voluntary organisation or in a registered children's home [*CA s 59(5)* and *Sch 6, para 10*]. In such cases the response is required from the voluntary organisation or person carrying on the home;

— a parent of any child above;

— any non-parent with parental responsibility for any child above;

— such other person as the authority, voluntary organisation or person carrying on the home consider has a sufficient interest in the child's welfare to warrant her/his representations being considered by them;

— a person exempted or seeking to be exempted under *Sch 7, para 4* (usual fostering limit) (see FOSTER PARENTS (23)); and

— a person qualifying for advice and assistance about the discharge of their functions by a local authority under *Part III* of the Act in relation to him.

10.7 **Inter-related procedures**

Representations made may have implications for other organisational procedures e.g. grievance or disciplinary hearings. The problem of concurrent investigations is not a new phenomenon, e.g. criminal investigation may be concurrent with disciplinary procedures, and the principles applicable should be the same. Clearly the complaint and any disciplinary action are separate matters and protection of the child should take priority. Where a complaint also calls for a disciplinary hearing it would normally be best for the disciplinary issue to be resolved first so that witnesses' statements and examination are taken with due care and formality. Consideration by an independent person with officers of the authority, even if allowed to interview witnesses, will not afford the same safeguards as the disciplinary procedure. Further, the authority's consequent response to a finding that a complaint is justified, could be nullified by later proceedings whose findings differed. It may be that a complainant would be prepared to withdraw or postpone representations until the issue of discipline is resolved. At the least, an authority's initial response in such cases may be that any action must await the outcome of disciplinary proceedings. Discussions with trade unions and staff side associations may lead to an agreed code or a method to resolve the handling of individual cases. The regulations require that oral representations received are put into writing and agreed with the complainant, and that the procedure is explained and assistance and guidance offered. The opportunity therefore exists at an early stage to reduce the potential complications.

10.8 Complaints and Representations

10.8 **Making the complaint**

The complaint may initially be oral or in writing. As outlined above, if made orally it must be put into writing and agreed with the complainant. The duty to act arises where a local authority receive any representations from an 'eligible' person (see 10.6 above). It is not easy to determine whether a 'statement' is intended as a 'complaint', requiring formal response. However a response in writing would normally help to determine such cases and this is called for in any event by the regulations where the 'complaint' is made orally. Written complaints should not normally be difficult to categorise as such, although the necessity, if taken literally, to consider with an independent person and respond to a 'non-critical statement concerning service to a child' is somewhat cumbersome and onerous.

10.9 Once a written complaint is received or an oral complaint is recorded in writing by the local authority and its accuracy agreed, an explanation of the procedure set out in the regulations must be sent to the complainant together with an offer of assistance and guidance or advice on where it may be obtained [*reg 4, SI 1991 No 894*].

Where the complainant is a person whose eligibility depends on the local authority considering s/he has a sufficient interest in the child's welfare to warrant consideration of her/his representations, the local authority must first decide that issue. If in favour, the complaint must be dealt with in the manner set out above, otherwise the local authority must notify her/him in writing accordingly that no further action will be taken and the child must also be notified of the result if 'appropriate having regard to his understanding'. A complaint may be withdrawn by the person making it at any stage, but there is no provision for informing the child concerned in *reg 7, (SI 1991 No 894)* or elsewhere, just as there is no provision for informing the child that a complaint has been made.

10.10 **Considering the complaint**

The local authority must, within 28 days of receipt of the complaint (or of the decision that a person has sufficient interest etc.), formulate a response and give notice in writing to the complainant, the child (if not her/himself the complainant and of sufficient understanding), the independent person and any other persons the authority considers have sufficient interest in the case [*regs 6 and 8, SI 1991 No 894*]. In practice it may be advisable to inform the child of what is being said in relation to her/him as otherwise the first knowledge of a complaint may be a written notice of the result of the local authority's consideration.

10.11 **The independent person**

The authority must appoint an 'independent person' to take part in the consideration of the complaint and s/he must take part in any discussions held about the action (if any) to be taken [*regs 5 and 6, SI 1991 No 894*]. 'Independent person' is defined as 'a person who is neither a member nor an officer of that authority' (the authority to whom the complaint is made). The DOH offers guidance on selection of independent persons and sounds a note of caution about selection of a member of a voluntary organisation when contractual arrangements exist between the authority and the organisation. (The DOH also offers guidance on the selection of spouses of excluded persons). The authority should bear in mind the racial and cultural aspects that may be involved when selecting an independent person for a particular complaint and indeed must be able to offer multi-lingual leaflets/notices or suitable assistance throughout the complaints procedure. The DOH guidance suggests that training and other supports such as legal advice may be appropriate. The procedure encompasses a co-ordinating officer, training and support of independent persons, written notifications, time limits, monitoring and further reference to a panel, all of which place a considerable burden on authorities irrespective of the merits of any particular complaint.

The independent person may wish to interview the child, complainant, parents, staff or other relevant persons in order to form a view, and questions of confidentiality and reimbursement of expenses will therefore arise. All of this should be covered in letters of appointment so that there is a clear understanding of duties and how they may be carried out, including access to case records. DOH guidance recommends the independent person be given access to relevant parts of the case record. This is unfortunate phrasing and suggests a degree of selectivity on the part of the authority. Concerns about confidentiality are understandable as there can be no satisfactory enforcement procedures and much will depend on the sensitivity of the individual and her/his training. However the judgment of what is relevant in a case record can hardly be made for independent persons if they are fully to play their role, and attempts to restrict access may be viewed with suspicion. Clearly a heavy responsibility will lie with the officer designated to assist the authority in the co-ordination of all aspects of the consideration of complaints. S/he must be able to deal with the sensibilities of staff as well as the independent person and carry sufficient weight to resolve potential disputes.

10.12 Which local authority deals with the complaint?

The Act requires every local authority to establish a procedure for considering complaints made to them *inter alia* by any child being looked after by them or who is in need but not so looked after and any local authority foster parent. As regards a child in need, services may be provided e.g. for a child in need resident in one area, by a local authority from another area. The complaint may relate to the delivery of those services and the Act and regulations afford no help in determining the appropriate authority. DOH guidance deals with complaints involving more than one authority and suggests the appropriate authority is where the child is being looked after or, in the case of other services, where the child normally resides as the responsibility for supplying services, accommodation or otherwise, to a child in need lies with the authority for the area where the child resides.

10.13 Notification to complainant and reference to panel

The local authority decides what to propose following consideration of the complaint, although the independent person is involved in any discussions and may have presented a written view. However, they must have regard to the findings of those considering the complaint [*CA s 26(7)*]. Notice of the result must be given within 28 days [*reg 8(1), SI 1991 No 894*] and (as with all notices under the regulations) must be in writing. The notice must inform the complainant of her/his right to have the matter referred to a panel. The complainant, if dissatisfied, may then, within 28 days of the date on which notice is given, ask for the matter to be referred to a panel.

10.14 Complaints and Representations

10.14 The panel, which must include at least one independent person, has to meet within 28 days of receipt of the request. They must consider any oral or written submissions that the complainant or authority wish to make and any oral or written submissions from the independent person appointed under *reg 5 (SI 1991 No 894)* if different from the independent person on the panel. The complainant may be accompanied by another person of her/his choice and may nominate that person to speak on her/his behalf. There are some arguments for involving a different independent person as panel member.

10.15 The panel must record their recommendations and reasons in writing within 24 hours of the meeting concluding, and notify the local authority, the complainant, any 'different' independent person and any other person the local authority considers has sufficient interest in the case [*reg 9(2), SI 1991 No 894*]. The child is not included in *reg 9(2), (SI 1991 No 894)* but by *CA 89, s 26(7)* where any representation has been considered under the procedure established by the section, the authority shall notify 'the child (if the authority consider he has sufficient understanding) . . . of the authority's decision in the matter, their reasons for taking that decision and . . . any action they have taken or propose to take'. While the panel's recommendations and reasons need not, it seems, be notified to the child, the authority's decisions will be. This contrasts with the provisions of *reg 8(1)* which does require the complainant and, if different, the person on whose behalf the representations were made, to be notified unless s/he is not of sufficient understanding and it would be likely to cause serious harm to her/his health or emotional condition. In most cases this will be the child although a foster parent, for example, might conceivably complain about the lack of support for parental visiting to a child.

10.16 The local authority then has to consider, with the independent panel member, what action (if any) to take and s/he must take part in any decisions about any such action. Due regard must be had to the panel recommendations [*CA s 26(7)*]. The regulations do not lay down a period within which the decision must be notified, but DOH guidance recommends 28 days. *Section 26(7)(b)* requires that reasons for the decision be communicated and it is suggested that the complainant should be advised of any other avenues of complaint or appeal that may be available.

10.17 **Monitoring the procedure** [*reg 10*]

A record of complaints received, their outcome and compliance with time limits must be kept. Annual reports have to be completed and these will be presented to the authority's Social Services Committee or, in the case of a voluntary organisation or registered home, be available at any inspection authorised by the Secretary of State. The DOH gives guidance on the contents of the report which should be 'anonymised' to preserve confidentiality and be open to inspection by the public.

10.18 **Voluntary organisations and registered children's homes**

As indicated above the regulations apply to accommodation provided by those homes where a child is not looked after by a local authority and references to the authority in this chapter refer in such a case to the voluntary organisation or person carrying on the home.

The definition of representations (including complaints) is modified so that representations are concerned with the discharge by the voluntary organisation of any of their functions under *s 61* in relation to the child (this section sets out the duties of voluntary organisations) and in the case of a registered home, in relation to the person carrying on the home the discharge of functions under *s 64*. *Section 64* sets out duties regarding the welfare of the child, and the different formulations are not significant. In both cases the complaint is confined to the discharge by the homes of the specific 'welfare' duties set out in *ss 61* and *64*.

10.19 **Complaints and appeals**

Application to the courts concerning local authority decisions under the *Children Act*, e.g. regarding contact under *s 34(3)*, may also be the subject of a complaint. The making of an application or appeal to the court while a complaint is also under consideration will present difficulties but is not ruled out by the legislation. The complainant may not wish to be interviewed, even by an independent person, and the authority may not wish to 'rehearse' its case before a panel. Neither reason is sufficient to defer or delay the consideration. Care should always be taken in formulating written notice of decisions and reasons irrespective of the knowledge of a pending application to the court. While consideration of the complaint may be less than complete, that will be at the choice of the complainant. The DOH guidance suggests legal advice be taken, but that relates to the care that should be taken rather than pointing to situations where the complaint can be deferred or rejected.

10.20 **Secretary of State's default powers**

Section 7D of the *Local Authority Social Services Act 1970* gives the Secretary of State power to declare an authority in default if satisfied that they have failed without reasonable excuse to comply with any of their duties which are social services functions other than a duty imposed by or under the *Children Act 1989*. Enforceable directions may then be given to ensure that that duty is complied with. *Section 84* of the 1989 Act gives the Secretary of State similar powers in relation to failure to comply with duties under the *Children Act 1989*. These powers relate to failure to comply with duties and not discretionary powers. The Secretary of State will need to be satisfied by cogent evidence that there has been a failure without reasonable excuse. There are few, if any, examples of the Secretary of State acting under *s 36* of the *National Assistance Act 1948* which also gave powers to find an authority in default (see *R v Kent CC and others ex parte Bruce, The Times*, 8 February 1986).

10.21 **Directions under Local Authority Social Services Act 1970, s 7B**

Complaints about local authority social services functions other than those dealt with under *s 26(3)* may be brought under the procedure in the directions. The section allows a complainant or anyone acting on her/his behalf, including, for example, a campaigning body (unlike the *s 26(3)* procedure) to make a complaint. The directions are mandatory and not guidance as issued under *s 7(1)* of the 1970 Act.

10.22 **Local Government Act 1974, Part IV**

A further method of processing a complaint against a local authority is via the Local Authority Commissioner, i.e. the 'Ombudsman'.

11 Consultation/Participation

11.1 References

See 11.3 below.

11.2 The requirement to consult and the need to encourage participation by adults and children in decision-making is a fundamental feature of the Act. This, together with the material listed in 11.3 below, means there can be few decisions regarding children in need, proposed to be adopted, looked after or proposed to be looked after by a local authority which do not require prior consultation with, participation by and notification to, the child and her/his parents, or non-parents having parental responsibility. There is also considerable emphasis on consultation with, and participation by, statutory and voluntary organisations.

11.3 Summary of relevant legislative and other provisions regarding consultation and participation.

(a) European Convention for the Protection of Human Rights and Fundamental Freedoms (Cmnd 8969) and cases before the European Court of Human Rights (see 11.4–11.6 below).

(b) European Convention on the Adoption of Children (Cmnd 3673) (see 11.7 below).

(c) Recommendation No R(87)6 of the Committee of Ministers to member states on foster families (see 11.8 below).

(d) Recommendation No R(84)4 of the Committee of Ministers to member states on parental responsibilities (see 11.8 below).

(e) European Social Charter (see 11.9 below).

(f) *Adoption Act 1976* (see 11.10 below).

(g) *Disabled Persons (Services, Consultation and Representation) Act 1986* (see 11.11 below).

(h) *Working Together* – DOH guidance on inter-agency co-operation – 'Cleveland' Inquiry recommendations on child abuse (see 11.12 below).

(j) *Children Act 1989*, and regulations thereunder (see 11.13–11.22 below).

11.4 EUROPEAN MATERIAL

The European Convention on Human Rights came into force on 3 September 1953. *Article 8* guarantees the right to respect for private and family life, home and correspondence. The UK has accepted an individual's right to petition the European Commission of Human Rights (after the legal remedies from a court within the UK have been exhausted). Once a complaint to the Commission is declared admissible, attempts are made to conciliate and achieve 'a friendly settlement'. If this fails, the Commission can refer the case to the European Court of Human Rights for a decision. The UK is bound to abide by the Court's judgment in any case to which it is a party. Unlike judgments of the Court of Justice of the European Communities, however, judgments of the Court of Human Rights are not directly enforceable in the UK courts. In *R v Secretary of State for the Home Department ex parte Brind [1990] 1 All ER 469 CA* it was said that the Convention had not been 'domesticated' and made part of English domestic law. The duty of the English courts 'is to decide disputes in accordance with English domestic law as it is, and not as it would be if full effect were given to this country's obligations under the treaty . . .'. English courts are not therefore normally concerned with the terms of the Convention, but the decisions of the Court of Human Rights have been implemented in the review and amendment of statute law, and new legislation in the main seeks to be consistent with the Convention. This is quite apparent in the *Review of Child Care Law*, a consultative document published by the Government in September 1985 and a precursor of the *Children Act 1989*.

11.5 In *W., B. and R. v UK (Judgments no 4/1986/102/150, 5/1986/103/151* and *6/1986/104/152)* the Court of Human Rights held there had been a breach of *Article 8*, because the parents of children in compulsory local authority care had been insufficiently involved in the authority's decision-making process, for example, by not being consulted in advance about the decision or being informed of it promptly. This was particularly evident in the way in which W's child was placed with long-term foster parents with a view to adoption and steps taken to terminate access by W and his wife. B's child was moved to long-term foster parents and access terminated, and R's parental rights were assumed, access terminated and the children placed for adoption.

It is worth noting that by the time the judgments were given, the *Child Care Act 1980* had been amended to afford a remedy that had not been available to the applicants at the time the local authority made the decision. Also, the Government had published a Code of Practice on access to children in care in 1983 giving support to the principles enunciated in the court's decision.

11.6 The influence of such decisions in changing English domestic law can also be seen in *Gaskin v UK (Case no 2/1988/146/200)*. The local authority was again found to be in breach of *Article 8*. Previously, English courts had refused the applicant access to his child care records. However, 1983 DHSS Circular no LAC(83)14 (now revoked) encouraged the view that people receiving personal social services should, subject to adequate safeguards, be able to discover what is said about them in social services records. The *Access to Personal Files Act 1987* and the regulations made thereunder [*Access to Personal Files (Social Services) Regulations 1989 (SI 1989 No 206)*] have, since April 1989, allowed individuals access to personal information about themselves held by a local authority for the performance of its social services functions (very much matching the provisions of the *Data Protection Act 1984*). Apart from any other justification, the need to harmonise with EC law on data protection was a factor influencing the latter Act.

11.7 European Convention on the Adoption of Children (Cmnd 3673) provides in *Article 9* that the competent authority shall not grant an adoption until appropriate enquiries have been made concerning *inter alia* the views of the child with respect to the proposed adoption.

11.8 The Recommendations and Resolutions of the Committee of Ministers of the Council of Europe are not binding on member governments but are formulated to further the aims of the Council, and the Committee may ask governments of member states to inform it of the action taken with regard to recommendations made.

Recommendation No R87(6) on foster families states (Principle 4) 'As far as possible before any important decision is taken concerning the person of the child, the foster parents should be given the opportunity to express their views', and (Principle 7) 'Before any decision is taken by the competent authority (on

11.9 Consultation/Participation

foster parents exercising parental responsibilities, or the removal of a child from foster parents) the parents and foster parents should be given the opportunity to express their views. The child should be consulted in his/her degree of maturity with regard to the decision so permits.'

Recommendation No R84(4) on parental responsibilities states (Principle 3) that where the competent authority is required to take a decision relating to the attribution of parental responsibilities or the way they are exercised and affecting the essential interests of the children, the latter should be consulted if their degree of maturity with regard to the decision so permits.

11.9 There is no provision for individuals to enforce the European Social Charter. Each of the contracting parties reports at two-yearly intervals on how the provisions it has accepted are being applied. Ultimately the Council of Europe parliamentary assembly may pass an 'opinion' on the report and the conclusion of a Committee of Experts, to the Council of Ministers, which can itself make recommendations to the states concerned.

Article 14 *The Right to Benefit from Social Welfare Services* (European Social Charter) states 'with a view to encourage the effective exercise of the right to benefit from social welfare services the contracting Parties undertake . . . (2) to encourage the participation of individuals and voluntary or other organisations in the establishment and maintenance of such services'.

11.10 The *Adoption Act 1976* states that in reaching any decision relating to the adoption of a child a court or adoption agency shall so far as practicable ascertain the wishes and feelings of the child regarding the decision and give due consideration to them having regard to her/his age and understanding [*AA s 6*].

Any decision relating to the adoption of a child does not, it would seem, include a decision on when agreement to adoption is being unreasonably withheld, nor a decision by a local authority as adoption agency to seek potential adopters for a child by advertisement (see *Re P (An Infant) Adoption: Parental Consent* [1977] 25 and *RB Kensington and Chelsea v K & Q* [1989] IFLR 399, and compare Lord Salmon *obiter* in *Re D (an infant) Adoption: Parental Consent 1977 AC 602*). See also as regards culture and religion *Adoption Rules 1984* and *Adoption Agency Regulations 1983 (SI 1983 No 1964)* (adoption agencies in placing a child must have regard (so far as is practicable) to any wishes of a child's parents and guardians as to religious upbringing of the child).

11.11 When ss 1–3 of the *Disabled Persons (Services, Consultation and Representation) Act 1986* are brought into force, an authorised representative of a disabled person will be able to act as that person's representative in connection with the exercise by a local authority of any of their functions under welfare enactments, to accompany the disabled person (otherwise than as her/his representative) to any meeting or interview in that respect and to receive information and inspect documents that the disabled person would be entitled to require the authority to supply to her/him. When the authority is making a decision on the provision of services, it must give the disabled person, or her/his authorised representative, an opportunity to make representations as to any needs, and if requested, an explanation of why the particular need cannot be met. The disabled person or her/his representative then has an opportunity to make further representations. Regulations (when made) may allow the authority itself to appoint a representative for a child looked after by them. Where the disabled child is under 16, her/his parents or a non-parent with parental responsibility may appoint a representative for her/him. A child under 16 will not be able to appoint her/his own representative.

Consultation/Participation 11.16

11.12 Both *Working Together* and a *Report of the Inquiry into Child Abuse in Cleveland 1987* (Cm 413) contain important advice and guidance which social workers in particular should follow.

11.13 **CHILDREN ACT 1989 AND REGULATIONS**

Consultation/co-operation between local authority and other agencies

When providing support for children and their families under *Part III* of the Act, a local authority may request the help of any health authority and any local education, housing or other local authority. A specific request must be met if it is 'compatible' with their own statutory or other duties and obligations and does not adversely prejudice the discharge of any of their functions [*CA 89 s 27*]. The Secretary of State may nominate other persons for the purposes of the section. Securing co-operation between statutory agencies may however be influenced by the budgetary requirements of both parties. An agency may wish to help but may not have the resources; if it is willing to help but also imposes a charge which cannot or would not be met then the principle of co-operation is of little practical value. *Section 29(9)* specifically allows a local authority complying with any request under this section, in relation to a child ordinarily resident in another area, to recover any expenses reasonably incurred. The omission of the Probation Service from the list of statutory agencies required to co-operate is also somewhat surprising, as they may well be involved with other family members. The rights of individual 'clients' of probation officers would have been protected by the proviso that the request for help is compatible with their own statutory duties etc.

11.14 *Section 22* of the *National Health Service Act 1977* imposes a duty on health and local authorities to co-operate 'in order to secure and advance the health and welfare of the people of England and Wales'. Under the Act, joint consultative committees were created to advise on the performance of the above duty and on the planning and operation of services of common concern to the authorities.

11.15 A local education authority may request assistance by way of provision of services for a child having special educational needs, from her/his local authority [*CA 89 s 27*]. Again such a request may cause difficulty if charges are raised or there is a difference of view as to the child's needs. *Section 27(4)* does not however make any proviso that the request does not unduly prejudice the discharge of any of the local authority functions. The allocation of social work time for a child with special educational needs may be a perfectly reasonable request, but unattainable in particular circumstances. In this respect, the Act is no more than a statement of principle with little or nothing to back up the expectations raised.

11.16 Consultation is required with local education authorities when a local authority are looking after a child and propose to place her/him in an establishment at which education is provided [*CA 89 s 28*]. The duty is to consult before placement so far as is reasonably practicable and notify once the placement is made and on termination. Inter-agency co-operation will not be effective unless arrangements are made for consultation and notification to be dealt with other than by the creation of a file or register and, while this comment is perhaps more pertinent to issues of child protection, the educational needs of children should not be understated or neglected. Under this section agencies will need to consider how and when information should be passed on e.g. as a child leaves the area of one education authority for another.

11.17 Consultation/Participation

11.17 Child protection

Section 47(9), (10) and *(11)* of the *Children Act 1989* make similar provision for co-operation between agencies in child protection cases. The list of agencies required to assist a local authority investigating whether a child is suffering, or is likely to suffer, significant harm is the same as in *s 27*. The omission of the police and probation service is unfortunate and seemingly disregards the recommendations of the *Cleveland Report* (Cm 413) that 'the police should develop, monitor and maintain communication and consultation with other agencies concerned with child protection' and 'the police should develop and practice inter-agency working including joint planning and interviews of children in investigation of sexual abuse within the family or caring agency'. All statutory agencies are enjoined by *Working Together* to co-operate and, if there is specific legislation as well as ministerial guidance, it is difficult to appreciate why the police and probation service have been left out, particularly as the duty to assist does not oblige any person to do so 'where doing so would be unreasonable in all the circumstances of the case'. The latter wording, quite different to the proviso in *s 27*, would seem to justify a refusal only if matters affecting the child and family made it unreasonable rather than the circumstances of the agency whose assistance is requested. That being so, the possible reticence of police officers in passing on information, for a time at least, during the conduct of an enquiry into a serious crime would be supported even if they were made subject to the section. Subject to any amendment of the Act, co-operation by the police and probation services is dependent solely on goodwill, mutual interest and ministerial guidance.

11.18 If the local authority investigation of suspected harm suggests that 'there are matters connected with the child's education which should be investigated', then there must be consultation with the relevant local education authority [*CA 89 s 47(5)*].

11.19 Partnership and consultation with a variety of bodies, statutory, voluntary and private will be required if local authorities are to take seriously their duty under *Sch 2, para 7* to 'take reasonable steps to encourage children not to commit criminal offences'. This is a broad commitment to crime prevention and could include seeking employment opportunities for young people as well as the organisation of leisure activities.

11.20 As regards day care services for pre-school and other children, a local authority must regularly review the provision they make under *s 18* (the extent to which child minding is available for children under eight and the provision of day care for under eights by private and voluntary organisations). The review must also include the provision made for under eights in hospitals, schools and other establishments which are exempted from registration by *Sch 9*. The first reviews must be within one year of the commencement of *s 19* (14 October 1991) and at least every three years thereafter. The review is to be conducted with the appropriate LEA and the authorities must have regard to any representations made to any one of them by any health authority and any other representations they consider to be relevant. The remit of the review must be published together with any proposals with respect to the matters reviewed. LEAs may be requested to assist the local authority in the exercise of their functions under *Part X* of the Act – *Childminding and Day Care* [*Sch 9 para 8*].

11.21 DOH guidance (Vol 2 Family Support, Day Care and Educational Provision for Young Children) urges that 'the local pattern and range of day care and related services for young children should be worked out at local level by local authorities in consultation with health authorities, voluntary organisations, employer interests, parents and other interested bodies and individuals'. Further, the guidance asks authorities to ensure that the review encourages debate about local services and how their development can produce benefits. Setting up the review and its conduct therefore calls for wide-ranging consultation and the participation of a broad range of interests.

11.22 Family support services generally (which include day care) also require the participation of voluntary organisations as well as others. Local authorities have a duty under *s 17(5)* to facilitate the provision by others of services which the authority have power to provide e.g. family support, day care, accommodation, and after care.

11.23 **Local authorities and the public at large**

The provision of family support services must be in the context of information on the need for those services. Authorities, then, must take reasonable steps to identify the extent to which there are children in need within their area, publish information about the services available from statutory and other bodies and seek to ensure that those who might benefit from the services receive the information relevant to them. Identifying the extent of need (which includes the needs of disabled children) may well involve consultation with relevant agencies or individuals in order to plan an appropriate range and level of response in collaboration with those able to provide services. Guidance stresses that the duty is corporate (although co-ordinated by a Social Services Department). Local authority grant aid powers will be particularly useful in encouraging and maintaining relevant local resources.

11.24 In order to provide services which are sensitive and relevant to the needs of different groups [*Sch 2 para 11*] special attention will have to be paid to what sections of the public themselves regard as important. Although *para 11* is confined to day care and fostering services, elsewhere the Act refers to cultural, religious and linguistic needs of children [*CA 89 s 22(5)*]. It would be unwise to plan provision for children and families without incorporating these dimensions in every aspect of service. That will involve, for example, supporting 'self-help' groups and actively seeking advice from various communities, organisations and individuals.

11.25 As mentioned above, 'encouraging children not to commit crime' can be seen as a broad community initiative, coupled with the duty to reduce the need to bring criminal, care and supervision proceedings [*Sch 2 para 7*]. An understanding and acceptance by the public of measures taken to provide alternatives and support of positive initiatives in leisure and recreational/counselling fields will be a prerequisite for success. The co-ordination of the various initiatives will also call for a continuing programme of consultation.

11.26 **Local authorities, parents and non-parents with parental responsibility**

Children 'accommodated' by a local authority are in a very different position from those formerly 'received into care'. The law is now clear – the authority does not acquire parental responsibility and, dependent upon the child's age and understanding, decisions from the mundane to the more important are to be made solely by those with parental responsibility or by those in agreement with such persons. Looking after a child (other than under a care order) then, necessarily involves agreement with parents and those with parental responsibility

11.27 Consultation/Participation

and as a corollary consultation with them before decisions are taken. This keynote of participation by adults in decision-making which flows from the concept of parental responsibility is reinforced by particular provisions of the Act in respect of all children looked after by a local authority whether under a care order or not.

11.27 Accommodation of a child is now a genuinely voluntary arrangement – parents can no longer be required to give notice before withdrawing from an arrangement, and authorities no longer have power to pass administrative resolutions to assume parental rights and duties. The reinforcement of this principle of consultation and participation mirrors the consideration of children's wishes and feelings in relation to the information given to them set out in 5.14 CHILD'S AGE AND UNDERSTANDING above.

11.28 **Specific provisions for consultation**

(a) Local authorities may not provide accommodation for a child under *s 20* if any person having parental responsibility for her/him who is willing and able to provide or arrange for accommodation objects [*CA 89 s 20(7)*].

It follows that unless a child has reached the age of 16 [*CA 89 s 20(11)*] the authority must consult those with parental responsibility about any proposal to accommodate if their plans are to be realised. Similarly, as such persons may remove a child from accommodation at any time [*CA s 20(8)*], plans for a phased return home, for example, must also be agreed. Local authorities cannot use *s 8* orders to overcome this, as *s 9(5)* prohibits the making of specific issue or prohibited steps orders to achieve a result which could be achieved by making a residence or contact order, and by *s 9(2)*, the authority cannot apply for, nor can a court make a residence or contact order in favour of a local authority (nor is wardship an option, see WARDSHIP (45)).

(b) Section 20(6) and the *Arrangements for Placement of Children (General) Regulations 1991 (SI 1991 No 890)* make it necessary for the authority to agree arrangements for the placement of a child looked after, but not in care, with a person with parental responsibility before the placement is made, and, if that is not practicable, as soon as may be thereafter. The arrangements must be recorded in writing, and, except in a care case, must include the matters specified in *Sch 4* to the regulations – in particular, the respective responsibilities of the authority, child and those with parental responsibility, any delegation of that responsibility to the authority and the arrangements for involving those persons (and the child) in decision-making. The Schedule also includes in the arrangements to be specified, the expected length of time or the steps which should apply to bring the arrangements to an end. All this will of course involve quite extensive consultation if agreement is to be reached.

(c) Once a child not in care has been placed the arrangements will dictate the way in which those with parental responsibility are involved in decision-making. The regulations mentioned above give flesh to the wording of the Act which requires the authority, before making any decision with respect to a child whom they are looking after or proposing to look after, to ascertain the wishes and feelings of those with parental responsibility (and the child). This duty under *s 22(4)* applies whether or not the child is in care. Those with parental responsibility for a child in care will not necessarily have a written record of the arrangements for involving them in decision-making. It is nevertheless important for such persons to have

Consultation/Participation 11.28

information about their 'rights' as well as duties when a child is subject to a care order. Having ascertained wishes and feelings the authority must give due consideration to them [*s 22(5)*].

(*d*) Local authorities must, subject to regulations, seek to place a child looked after by them with a parent or non-parent with parental responsibility (or where in care, with any person in whose favour a residence order was in force immediately before the care order was made). This again requires consultation and the duty is excluded only if not reasonably practicable or consistent with the child's welfare, or, if the child is subject to a care order, the placement is not in accordance with *The Placement of Children with Parents etc. Regulations 1991 (SI 1991 No 893)*.

If the child in care is placed with a parent etc. the regulations impose a duty on the local authority to seek to reach agreement on certain matters, and the placement is not to be put into effect unless and until such an agreement has been reached and recorded in writing.

(*e*) Parents and those with parental responsibility must be informed of where a child looked after by a local authority is placed unless the child is in care and the authority has reasonable cause to believe that informing the person would prejudice the child's welfare [*CA Sch 2 para 15*].

(*f*) The Act is more explicit than previous legislation in defining the limits of parental responsibility when a child is in local authority care. Under the *CYPA 1969* a care order gave the local authority 'the same powers and duties . . . as his parent or guardian'. Now the local authority acquires parental responsibility (without extinguishing the responsibility of others) but may not use it to determine the extent to which a parent may meet her/his responsibilities unless it is necessary to do so to safeguard or promote the child's welfare *s 33(4)*. The effect of this provision is again to emphasise the need for adequate consultation about decisions with those having parental responsibility and highlights the need for well prepared 'care plans'.

(*g*) Courts, before making a care order, will consider the arrangements made or proposed for contact. Prior consultation will be essential. Regulations do not require arrangements regarding placement including contact to be agreed beforehand if the child is to be in care, but proposals for contact which have not been discussed with parents are likely to meet with strong reactions from the courts.

(*h*) The duty to provide accommodation for children whom they are looking after requires the local authority to place the child with a parent or non-parent with parental responsibility, or where the child is in care a person in whose favour a residence order was made immediately before the making of the care order, or 'a relative, friend or other person connected with him' (where a child is in care such a placement may only be made in accordance with *The Placement of Children with Parents etc. Regulations 1991 (SI 1991 No 893)*). Extensive consultation is therefore required (quite apart from the question of agreeing arrangements) in order to assess the suitability of a potentially wide number of persons before, for example, considering a foster placement.

(*j*) *Section 26(2)(d)* and the *Review of Children's Cases Regulations 1991 (SI 1991 No 895)* impose a duty to seek the views of (the child), parents or non-parents with parental responsibility and to notify the results of the

11.28 Consultation/Participation

review. If the six-monthly reviews are to be conducted efficiently, preparations for ascertaining the views of parents etc. will need to be made and also for their involvement in the review whether by attendance or otherwise. These are onerous provisions which could work more effectively if there were regular consultation with the persons to be involved and they were kept well informed before reviews (and afterwards as required by the regulations).

(k) *Regulations 15, 16* and *17* of the *Children (Secure Accommodation) Regulations 1991 (SI 1991 No 1505)* require the local authority to inform *inter alia* the appointed independent visitor of their intentions to apply to the court to keep the child in secure accommodation and for that person's wishes and feelings to be taken into account when such accommodation is reviewed.

12 Conduct of Children's Homes

12.1 References

Children Act 1989, Schs 4, 5 and *6*
Children's Homes Regulations 1991 (SI 1991 No 1506)
Department of Health guidance Vol 4 Residential Care
Arrangements for Placement of Children (General) Regulations 1991 (SI 1991 No 890)
Review of Children's Cases Regulations 1991 (SI 1991 No 895)

12.2 BACKGROUND

The 1989 Act (*Parts VI, VII* and *VIII* and *Schs 4, 5* and *6*) deal respectively with community, voluntary and registered children's homes. Previous regulations have been superseded by modifications and the main changes in the law are:

— private children's homes are now registered with and inspected by the local authority (the *Children's Homes Act 1982* which would have had the same effect was never brought into force and has now been repealed)

— all homes are subject to the same or similar provisions

— all homes now have to provide a statement of their objectives

— corporal punishment is prohibited.

The Schedules deal principally with registration of homes and the instruments of management for controlled and assisted community homes. *Parts I, II* and *III* of the regulations, affecting conduct and administration of the homes, apply to all homes. *Part VIII* of the Act relates to local authority visits to registered and voluntary homes. *Part VI* applies to community homes, *Part VII* to voluntary homes (registration) and *Part VIII* to registered homes (registration). Residential care, nursing and mental nursing homes accommodating four or more children are not governed by the regulations as they are excluded from the definition of registered children's or voluntary homes. (They are dealt with under the *Registered Homes Act 1984*.) When the *Registered Homes (Amendment) Act 1991* is brought into force, homes accommodating three or less disabled children will also be liable to register under the 1984 Act unless exempted by the Secretary of State. This is likely to be the case in order to avoid also having to register under the 1989 Act.

12.3 CONDUCT OF THE HOMES

This part of the regulations prescribes in detail the nature and quality of the accommodation, equipment and catering facilities in all homes. The following are not exhaustive of the requirements imposed [*SI 1991 No 1506, regs 4 to 14*].

12.4 A statement of objectives available for inspection by the persons specified in the Schedule will set out *inter alia* the experience of staff in the home, arrangements for contact with parents, relatives and friends, arrangements for religious observance, methods of control and discipline and arrangements for reviews and dealing with 'representations'.

12.5 Conduct of Children's Homes

12.5 The authority responsible for the home must ensure that the number of staff, their experience and qualifications are adequate to safeguard and promote the welfare of children accommodated. Staffing complements should be based on the needs of the children in the home and the task assigned to the home but the DOH guidance does not specify any staff ratios. Guidance on the lines of 'Home Life' dealing with adult residential care is being prepared by the National Institute of Social Work in collaboration with the 'Wagner Development Group' and is expected to be available in 1992 (see paras 1.27–1.53 DOH guidance Vol 4 for more details).

12.6 Accommodation should include facilities for a child to meet privately with parents, friends, solicitors, GALs and others, for a child to launder her/his own clothes if s/he wishes to do so, and for pay-phones to enable calls to be made and received in private.

12.7 **Control and discipline** (DOH guidance Vol 4 paras 1.81–1.91; *reg 8, SI 1991 No 1506*)

Subject to the directions of the Secretary of State in respect of particular children, the only disciplinary measures to be used are those 'for the time being approved by the responsible authority' for the home.

12.8 Certain measures cannot be used unless necessary to prevent injury to people or serious damage to property, or arising from court orders or the instructions of registered medical/dental practitioners to protect the health of a child. The responsible authority may also impose, for example, certain conditions on contact, otherwise forbidden, to protect the welfare of the child, without a court order. *Schedule 2* to the 1989 Act requires a local authority looking after a child to promote contact between the child, parents, persons with parental responsibility and any relative, friend and other person connected with them unless it is not reasonably practicable or consistent with the child's welfare. Subject, then, to any order for contact with a particular individual, the authority could prohibit or impose conditions on contact with, for example, a relative or friend without seeking a court order.

12.9 The measures (subject to the above which cannot be used) are as follows.

(*a*) Any form of corporal punishment. The DOH guidance includes in this rough handling, throwing missiles and slapping, but does not include 'holding' although physical restraint should be used rarely and only to prevent a child harming her/himself or others or from damaging property.

(*b*) The deprivation of food and drink.

(*c*) Any restriction on visits to or by any child or any restriction on or delay in communications by telephone or post with parents, non-parents with parental responsibility, relatives and friends, any independent visitor, assigned social worker, GAL, any solicitor acting for the child and whom the child wishes to instruct.

(*d*) Any requirement that a child wear distinctive or inappropriate clothes (unless school or scout uniform, for example).

(*e*) The use or withholding of medication, or medical or dental treatment.

(*f*) The intentional deprivation of sleep.

(*g*) While the imposition of fines (except by way of reparation) and sanctions such as docking part of pocket money are permitted, it is suggested that

Conduct of Children's Homes 12.17

these measures should be restricted to cases of willful damage, for example, and should not exceed two-thirds of the allowance.

(h) Any intimate physical examination of the child. This would outlaw physical search for drugs by home staff, for example, although search of clothing may be necessary from time to time, not as a punishment but as a safety measure.

(j) Physical restriction of liberty. The *Children (Secure Accommodation) Regulations 1991 (SI 1991 No 1505)*, prohibits the use of accommodation to restrict the liberty of a child being looked after by a local authority in premises which have not been approved for such use by the Secretary of State (see SECURE ACCOMMODATION (42)).

12.10 A child should be enabled to attend services and to receive instruction and observe any requirements (whether as to dress, diet or otherwise) of her/his religious persuasion.

12.11 There should be a choice for each course of each main meal, and facilities for children to prepare their own meals if they wish. Any special dietary need due to health, religion, racial origin or cultural background must be met.

12.12 Children should be able to purchase clothes according to their needs. This should be done on an individual basis through normal shopping arrangements. There is no place generally for bulk buying or special purchasing arrangements.

12.13 ADMINISTRATION OF HOMES

Arrangements for medical examinations, written health assessments and education are governed by the *Arrangements for Placement of Children Regulations 1991* and the *Review of Children's Cases Regulations 1991* (see COMMUNITY HOMES (9) and REVIEWS (38)). The placement regulations also require a written case record for each child to be compiled.

12.14 The *Children's Homes Regulations* require in addition an individual case record to be kept in the home. The details to be included are set out in *Sch 2* to the regulations.

12.15 The other records which must be kept are set out in *Sch 3* and relate not only to admissions and discharges, but *inter alia*, qualifications of staff, residents, fire drills, medicinal products administered, punishments, money deposited by children, menus and daily rosters.

12.16 *Regulation 19* defines significant events which include improper conduct by a member of staff and serious harm to a child which must be notified to parents etc., the local authority where the home is situated, the registration authority and in certain circumstances the Secretary of State.

12.17 Local authority visits

Every child placed in a voluntary or registered home in their area, not being looked after by a local authority, must be visited within 28 days of being notified of the placement. Notification is required by *reg 5* of the *Arrangement for Placement of Children (General) Regulations 1991* (see COMMUNITY HOMES (9)). Visits are also required within 14 days of a request from the home or 7 days if informed that the child's welfare may be at risk.

12.18 Conduct of Children's Homes

12.18 Further visits may be needed from time to time but there is an obligation to visit 6 months after the first visit following notification of the placement of a child, and within 28 days where a child remains in accommodation which the authority are not satisfied is safeguarding the child's welfare.

12.19 The visitor should see the child alone, read all records and make a written report at every visit.

12.20 CHILD ABUSE IN HOMES

Procedures integrated with those of the Area Child Protection Committee are needed for each home which together with appropriate training will ensure that staff recognise and deal with abuse in accordance with DOH guidance and local authority policies.

13 Contact

13.1 References

Children Act 1989, ss 8, 22, 34, 43, 44 and 46
Arrangements for Placement of Children (General) Regulations 1991 (SI 1991 No 890)
Review of Children's Cases Regulations 1991 (SI 1991 No 895)
Contact with Children Regulations 1991 (SI 1991 No 891)
Children (Representations, Placements and Reviews) (Miscellaneous Amendments) Regulations 1991 (SI 1991 No 2033)

13.2 BACKGROUND AND DEFINITION

The relevant matrimonial, guardianship and child care legislation no longer refers to 'access' to children by parents and others. The concept has been replaced by 'contact'. Access was not defined in previous legislation and was generally regarded as 'the right to see' a child. Contact does not in the context of the Act have such a limited meaning. A contact order under *s 8* means 'an order requiring the person with whom a child lives, or is to live, to allow the child to visit or stay with the person named in the order, or for that person and the child otherwise to have contact with each other'. That should be taken to mean in the colloquial sense, corresponding, telephoning as well as what used to be known as 'staying access' over a short period (see Law Commission Paper No 172). Contact order is defined as above but 'contact', as in the local authority duty to promote and maintain contact, is not so defined. However, it would be unwise to seek to limit the meaning of contact in any context to the physical act of meeting. So, for example, in considering the local authority duty to allow reasonable contact with a child subject to a care order, regard must be had to all forms of communication between the child and, for example, her/his parents.

13.3 GENERAL PRINCIPLES

Consultation

Ascertaining the wishes and feelings of the child and others before any decision is made is a fundamental duty of local authorities. This duty extends not only to children accommodated or in care but also to children whom it is proposed to accommodate or take into care under a care order. Certainly the duty extends to consideration of contact arrangements and, as a child is party to care proceedings, s/he will be invited by the court to comment on the proposals for contact before a care order is made.

Promotion of contact

The local authority looking after a child is under a duty to promote contact with parents, non-parents with parental responsibility and any relative, friend or other person connected with her/him. In carrying out that duty the authority has to take reasonable steps to ensure that persons with parental responsibility are kept informed of where the child is accommodated. Correspondingly, every such person has to keep the authority informed of her/his address. If the

13.4 Contact

authority has reasonable cause to believe that informing anybody of the whereabouts of a child in care would prejudice her/his welfare they are not bound to do so.

Promotion of contact is assisted by the duty in *s 23(7)* to place a child near her/his home and together with any siblings so far as reasonably practicable and consistent with her/his welfare. Further, *Sch 2, para 16* gives the authority power to pay expenses incurred in making contact by the child or others where a visit could not otherwise be made without undue financial hardship.

13.4 CHILD ACCOMMODATED BY A LOCAL AUTHORITY

Parental responsibility and contact

A local authority providing accommodation for a child other than under a care order (and for limited purposes under an emergency protection order where a separate provision is made), (see EMERGENCY PROTECTION OF CHILDREN (20)) does not acquire parental responsibility. It follows that the authority has no power to limit or refuse contact, its duty is to 'endeavour to promote contact'. Furthermore, under the *Arrangements for Placement of Children (General) Regulations 1991 (SI 1991 No 890)* the local authority must agree with a person with parental responsibility before placement unless impracticable, the arrangements for contact with parents, non-parents with parental responsibility, any relative, friend, or other person connected with the child. This formal agreement does not supersede the requirement to consult the child and others prior to making any decision regarding placement [*s 22(4)*]. The agreement must be notified in writing to any person entitled to be consulted prior to the decision-making about children [*SI 1991 No 890, reg 5*] – normally the child, her/his parents and non-parents with parental responsibility.

Written agreements will therefore replace the discretion which local authorities have hitherto exercised, subject only to the DOH guidance in Vol 3 Ch 6, and will be based on prior consultation regarding the wishes of the child, parents and non-parents with parental responsibility. The new guidance emphasises the fact that good contact is to be presumed and the regulations require the reasons why contact with any person referred to above would not be reasonably practicable or would be inconsistent with the child's welfare to be specified in writing. *Schedule 2 para 16* gives the local authority power to meet travelling, subsistence or other expenses of such persons in visiting the child. The welfare of the child may require that s/he be accommodated even though agreement on contact cannot be reached. It will be possible for the parent (or the child with leave) to apply for a *s 8* contact order to define contact. By *s 9(2)* no application for a contact order, for example, to define contact may be made by a local authority.

Reviews

The *Review of Children's Cases Regulations 1991 (SI 1991 No 895)* require that a child accommodated by a local authority is informed at each review of her/his right to apply with leave for a *s 8* order (for example residence or contact). Further the local authority must consider the arrangements for contact having regard to their duty to endeavour to promote contact with parents, non-parents with parental responsibility and any relative, friend, or other person connected with her/him and whether there is any need for changes in the arrangements made in order to promote contact with her/his family. Case records for the child must contain details of the arrangements for contact and contact orders.

Before making any decision to change contact arrangements the local authority must, so far as practicable, ascertain the wishes and feelings of the child, his parents, non-parents with parental responsibility and any other person whose wishes and feelings the authority consider to be relevant [*s 22(4)*].

Care orders – consultation

Before making a care order the court is required to (a) consider the arrangements which the authority have made, or propose to make, for affording any person contact with the child; and (b) invite the parties to the proceedings to comment on those arrangements. In effect much the same consultation is required prior to the making of an order as for the proposed placement of a child to be accommodated, although the *Arrangements for Placement of Children (General) Regulations* do not in the case of a child in care require agreement with a person with parental responsibility, nor do details of contact arrangements have to be included in the written notice of arrangements.

While the child is subject to a care order the authority must allow reasonable contact with her/his parents, any guardian and any person in whose favour a residence order was in force immediately before the making of a care order.

The basic assumption of reasonable contact discussed in court before the making of a care order will not be appropriate in all circumstances. The court of its own motion may make an order for contact under *s 34* regarding contact with any person when making a care order, or at any family proceedings in connection with a child in the care of a local authority.

The authority or the child may apply for an order at any time defining the contact to be allowed between the child and any named person. Parents, any guardian and any person who has a residence order in her/his favour immediately before the making of the care order, and any person with the leave of the court may also apply at any time for contact between them and the child to be defined. A parent's right to apply for contact is no longer limited to circumstances where the local authority has refused or terminated access. Repeated applications for contact are limited by *s 91(17)* which provides that where an application has been refused there must be an interval of at least six months before another application may be made, unless the leave of the court has been obtained.

Contact arrangements must be considered in reviews of the child (*Sch 1* of the *Review of Children's Cases Regulations 1991*). The local authority is required to explain to the child any steps s/he may take under the act. That requirement is essential if the child is to be enabled to express her/his wishes and feelings effectively.

Refusal of contact

Contact ordered under *s 34* may be refused for up to seven days if it is a matter of urgency, and the local authority are satisfied it is necessary to safeguard or promote the child's welfare [*s 34(6)*]. Where contact has been refused the authority must notify the child, if of sufficient understanding, her/his parents, any guardian, person who held a residence order or had care by virtue of an order in the exercise of the High Court's inherent jurisdiction immediately before the care order was made, or any other person whose wishes and feelings are considered to be relevant [*Contact with Children Regulations 1991 (SI 1991 No 891), reg 2*].

13.5 Contact

Departure from terms of s 34 order

By agreement with the person in relation to whom the order is made the local authority may depart from the terms of the order, provided that where the child is of sufficient understanding, s/he also agrees, and written notice is sent to the persons mentioned above of the decision, reasons for the decision, duration, and remedies available in case of dissatisfaction [*SI 1991 No 891, reg 3* and *Sch*].

Variation/suspension of contact arrangements

Where a child is not in care (and therefore no order under *s 34* has been made) the arrangements made for contact are by agreement with the local authority and are set out in writing. These arrangements may be varied or suspended but then written notice to the persons mentioned above must be given as soon as the decision is made containing as much of the information set out in CONSULTATION/PARTICIPATION (11) as the authority considers they need to know.

13.5 Section 8 contact order

Any court hearing family proceedings (which includes care proceedings) may make a *s 8* contact order whether on its own motion or on application. The ability of certain persons to intervene in existing family proceedings as of right or with leave of the court means, for example, that in the course of care proceedings the court may hear applications for a *s 8* contact order or decide to make one of its own motion. A *s 8* order may now also be applied for in the course of adoption proceedings and this is an entirely new right of intervention.

The following persons are able to intervene and seek a contact order as of right:

(*a*) any parent or guardian of the child;

(*b*) any person in whose favour a residence order is in force with respect to the child;

(*c*) any party to a marriage whether or not in relation to whom the child is a child of the family;

(*d*) any person with whom the child has lived for a period of at least three years;

(*e*) any person who

   (i) in any case where a residence order is in force in respect of a child, has the consent of each of the persons in whose favour the order was made;

   (ii) in any case where the child is in the care of a local authority has the consent of the authority; or

   (iii) in any other case has the consent of each of those (if any) who have parental responsibility for the child.

(*f*) any other person may intervene with leave of the court.

Applications may also be made independently of any other proceedings in being i.e. a 'free-standing application'. The same persons as above have a right to make free-standing applications and others may apply with leave of the court. Further, Rules of Court may prescribe categories of person entitled to apply.

13.6 A number of restrictions are imposed by the Act.

(a) Where the child her/himself applies for leave to apply, the court may only grant leave if satisfied that s/he has sufficient understanding to make the proposed application.

(b) Where the person applying for leave is not the child concerned the court shall have particular regard to

   (i) the nature of the proposed application;

   (ii) the applicants connection with the child;

   (iii) any risk of the proposed application disrupting the child's life to such an extent that s/he would be harmed by it; and

   (iv) where the child is being accommodated by a local auhtority (N.B. the court may not make a *s 8* contact order if the child is in care) the authority's plans for the child's future and the wishes and feelings of the child's parents.

(c) The period of three years in paragraph (d) above need not be continuous but must not have begun more than five years before or ended more than three months before the making of the application.

(d) A person who is, or was, at any time within the six months preceding the application, a local authority foster parent may not apply for leave unless

   (i) s/he has the consent of the authority;

   (ii) s/he is a relative of the child; or

   (iii) the child has lived with her/him for at least three years preceding the application. (The period of three years need not be continuous but must have begun not more than five years before the making of the application.)

(e) The contact order may not have effect beyond the age of 16 unless the court is satisfied that the circumstances of the case are exceptional.

(f) No contact order may be made with respect to a child who has reached the age of 16 years unless the court is satisfied the circumstances of the case are exceptional.

(g) A local authority cannot apply for a contact order and no such order can be made in favour of one.

(h) A contact order requiring a parent with whom the child lives to visit or otherwise have contact with the other parent shall cease to have effect if the parents live together for a continuous period of more than six months.

13.7 Directions

The order may contain directions of the court about its implementation and impose conditions which must be complied with by parents and others. The order or directions may be for a specified period and may contain such incidental, supplemental or consequential provisions as the court thinks fit [*s 11(7)*].

13.8 Child assessment orders, emergency protection orders and police protection

If a child assessment order specifies removal from home the order must specify contact with such other persons as the court thinks fit.

13.8 Contact

An emergency protection order may contain directions on contact which is, or is not allowed between the child and named persons, but subject to that the applicant for the order must allow reasonable contact with parents, non-parents with parental responsibility, any person with whom the child was living immediately before the order, anyone with the right to contact (under a *s 34*, or *s 8* order) and any person acting on behalf of any of the above. Where a child is in police protection, the designated officer must allow, so far as is reasonable and in the child's best interest, contact with parents, non-parents with parental responsibility, any person with whom the child was living immediately before being taken into police protection, any person with rights to contact (under a *s 34*, or *s 8* order) and any person acting on behalf of the above.

14 Contributions Towards Maintenance

14.1 References

Children Act 1989, Part III and *Sch 2*

14.2 LIABILITY TO CONTRIBUTE – CHILD LOOKED AFTER BY A LOCAL AUTHORITY

Where a child is looked after by a local authority (other than under an interim care order, detained under *s 53* of the *Children and Young Persons Act 1933*, or removed under *CA 1989, s 21* (removal under *Part V*, in police protection, on remand or subject to a supervision order with residence requirement)) consideration must be given to recovering contributions towards the child's maintenance. Contributions are only recoverable if the local authority considers it reasonable to do so.

14.3 WHO PAYS?

The persons liable to contribute are each of the parents of a child under 16, and where s/he has reached 16, the child her/himself. However, a parent is not liable to contribute while in receipt of income support or family credit. The DOH takes the view that liability is suspended for the period income support is received, not avoided permanently. Nor is there any liability while the child is allowed to live with a parent.

14.4 Agreement on contributions

In order to recover contributions the local authority must serve a 'contribution notice' in writing specifying a weekly sum (no greater than would be paid for a similar child to a local authority foster parent) that it considers reasonable having regard to the contributors' means. The notice must also specify the arrangements for payments, including the date liability begins, the date contributions are to begin and the date of the first payment. Liability begins no earlier than the date of notice. 'Flat rate' contributions are permitted, so that an authority may specify a weekly sum which is a standard contribution for all children they are looking after [*Sch 2 para 22*].

14.5 Where the authority and contributor agree the sum, which the contributor is to contribute and arrangements for payment (whether as specified in the contribution notice or otherwise) and the contributor acknowledges this in writing, any sum due and unpaid is recoverable as a civil debt.

14.6 Contribution orders

If agreement is not reached within one month of service of the contribution notice or notice withdrawing her/his agreement is served by the contributor, the authority may seek an order from the court. The court cannot exceed the sum specified in the contribution notice and must have regard to means [*Sch 2 para 23*].

14.7 Orders may be varied or revoked and agreement on a fresh contribution notice discharges the order. Such agreement must be notified to the court.

14.8 Contributions Towards Maintenance

14.8 **Enforcement**

On request, sums agreed and ordered to be paid may be collected and enforced by an authority where the contributor is currently living. The authority will have to agree any deductions for services rendered.

14.9 The Secretary of State is empowered [*Sch 2 para 25*] to make regulations as to the procedures for reaching agreements with contributors and 'collecting authorities' and the considerations to be had in deciding what is a reasonable sum and what the arrangements for payment should be.

15 Court Structure

15.1 References

Children Act 1989, s 92
Family Proceedings Courts (Constitution) Rules 1991 (SI 1991 No 1405)
Family Proceedings Courts (Constitution) (Metropolitan Area) Rules 1991 (SI 1991 No 1426)
The Children (Allocation of Proceedings) Order 1991 (SI 1991 No 1677)

15.2 The Act establishes a new court structure which aims to provide a unified system for dealing with cases and a more flexible approach. It comprises three tiers.

   (a) *The family proceedings court.* This replaces the old magistrates domestic court which heard cases concerning children and maintenance and the civil jurisdiction of juvenile courts. In future the juvenile court will be concerned only with criminal cases. The court will be staffed by magistrates drawn from the 'family panel' for each petty sessional area or in some cases, where combined panels exist, from two petty sessional areas. Separate arrangements exist for Inner London and the City of London, which are combined to form one panel. [The *Family Proceedings Courts (Constitution) Rules 1991 (SI 1991 No 1405)* and the *Family Proceedings Courts (Constitution) (Metropolitan Area) Rules 1991 (SI 1991 No 1426)*].

   (b) *County courts.* There are now four classes of county courts.

   (i) Non-designated county courts. These deal with civil cases e.g. actions for damages, debt, housing and so on. They also have jurisdiction to hear cases brought under the *Domestic Violence and Matrimonial Proceedings Act 1976* which may involve consideration of children and which are classed as family proceedings under the Act (see FAMILY PROCEEDINGS (22)). If an application for an injunction involves a contested application for say a *s 8* order then that should be transferred to a family hearing centre. If such an application involved an application for a care order then it should be transferred to a care centre. This might arise where the judge had ordered a *s 37* investigation (see 20.3), for example.

   (ii) Divorce county courts. All divorce, judicial separation proceedings and those to annul a marriage must be started at a divorce county court. Where they develop into care proceedings or contested *s 8* applications they should be transferred to either a care centre or a family hearing centre.

   (iii) Family hearing centres. In England and Wales, 102 county courts have been designated family hearing centres. They are able to deal with applications under *Parts I* and *II* of the Act, which includes applications for *s 8* orders. The plan is that all contested *s 8* applications heard at county court level will be heard at family hearing centres. Adoption applications which have been issued in or transferred to a county court will be heard by a family hearing centre if they are opposed. Family hearing centres cannot hear care proceedings which must be heard by care centres.

   (iv) Care centres. Applications under *Parts II, IV*, or *V* of the Act which are to be heard in a county court must be heard at a care

15.3 Court Structure

centre. This includes all care proceedings transferred from family proceedings courts and any family proceedings begun in a county court where an application is made under those parts of the Act. Each petty sessions area has a care centre allocated to it.

The Principal Registry of the Family Division, based at Somerset House in London, has been designated a divorce county court, a family hearing centre and a care centre. A complete list of the designations given to each county court is set out in *SI 1991 No 1677*.

(c) *The High Court*. The Family Division of the High Court can deal with all cases under the Act which have either been started in the High Court or transferred to it.

15.3 WHERE PROCEEDINGS START

In general terms applications by local authorities must start in the family proceedings court. Applications which do not involve local authorities can normally be made in either the family proceedings court, the county court or the High Court. There are a number of exceptions to this which are set out below. It is also important to remember that proceedings can be transferred from one court to another. The circumstances in which this can happen are listed in 15.4 TRANSFER OF PROCEEDINGS below.

Cases which must start in the family proceedings court

The following must be started in a family proceedings court:

— applications for secure accommodation orders (see SECURE ACCOMMODATION (42));

— applications for or concerning care and supervision orders;

— applications concerning care contact orders;

— applications for permission to change a child's name or remove a child in care from the United Kingdom and those made under *Sch 2, para 19* (approval for a child in local authority care to live abroad);

— applications for education supervision orders;

— applications for child assessment orders;

— applications for and concerning emergency protection orders;

— applications for an order to assist in the discovery of children;

— applications for recovery orders;

— applications for the recovery of children in an emergency;

— *s 77(1)* and *s 102* applications;

— applications for contribution orders;

— appeals under *Sch 8, para 8*;

— applications under *s 21* of the *Adoption Act 1976* (transfer of parental rights and duties between adoption agencies).

However, applications for care, supervision, education supervision, child assessment or emergency or recovery orders, which are made as a result of a direction

Court Structure 15.4

under *s 37* must be made in the High Court or a care centre. This means that if a family proceedings court orders an investigation under *s 37* in family proceedings, any of the applications referred to above which are made as a result of that cannot be made in the family proceedings court. Where an application is made for secure accommodation, care or supervision, leave to change name, leave to remove from the United Kingdom, approval of arrangements for a child to live abroad, care contact, education supervision, emergency protection, discovery, recovery or police assistance orders and there are already existing proceedings of the same kind in another court the application must be made to that court.

Cases which must start in the county court

— applications made as a result of a *s 37* investigation;
— applications made in divorce proceedings for *s 8* orders must be started in the divorce county court where the divorce is being dealt with.

15.4 TRANSFER OF PROCEEDINGS

Criteria for transfers

When deciding whether or not to transfer the proceedings to another court, the court must take the following into account:

— whether transfer would delay or significantly accelerate the proceedings, bearing in mind that delay is generally detrimental to the child;
— the complexity or difficulty of the factors or the evidence in the case;
— the number of parties;
— any conflict between the law of England and Wales and that of another jurisdiction;
— the novelty or difficulty of the point of law;
— whether or not there is a point of general public interest;
— whether it would be appropriate for the proceedings to be heard with other family proceedings pending in another family court.

Procedure for transfers

The court can transfer proceedings either of its own volition or at the request of one of the parties.

Transfers to different levels of the court system

Most proceedings can be transferred to a different level of court but some cannot. See the *Children (Allocation of Proceedings) Order 1991 (SI 1991 No 1677)*.

16 Cross Border Transfers

16.1 **References**

Social Work Scotland Act 1968, ss 72, 73, 74 and 75
Children and Young Persons Act 1969, ss 25 and 26
Children Act 1989, s 101

16.2 **INTRODUCTION**

Previous legislation on the transfer of care and supervision orders has remained in force. However, power is taken to prescribe by regulations as regards transfers between England and Wales and Northern Ireland, the Channel Islands or the Isle of Man, a singular updated framework for the identification of all the orders made by courts which may be transferred, with any necessary consequential amendments to the *Children and Young Persons Act 1969* or modifications of the *Children Act 1989*.

16.3 **Transfers to and from Scotland**

The statutory scheme applies where the parent of a child subject to a relevant order resides or proposes to reside in Scotland, or England and Wales, or Northern Ireland.

16.4 **Care orders**

The local authority (or *Minister of Home Affairs* for Northern Ireland) may refer the subject of a care order to the reporter for the area where the parent will reside, who will then arrange a children's hearing under *Part III* of the *Social Work Scotland Act 1968*. Once the case is disposed of, the original order ceases to have effect.

Care orders made, or deemed to be made, under the *Children Act 1989* may be so transferred (i.e. orders under the *CYPA 1969* continued in force by virtue of the *Children Act 1989, Sch 14*).

16.5 A child in a residential establishment under a supervision requirement of the 1968 Act may be referred to the Secretary of State by a children's hearing. The Secretary of State may then commit the child to the care of the local authority where the parent resides.

16.6 Transfer of supervision orders are dealt with by application to a children's hearing or court. The necessary amendments to the 1968 Act to allow for existing or new orders to be transferred are in *Sch 13* of the 1989 Act and *Sch 16* of the *Courts and Legal Services Act 1990*.

16.7 **Transfers between England and Wales and Northern Ireland, Channel Islands and Isle of Man**

Care orders (or their counterpart order) under the 1969 legislation may be transferred and regulations to be made under *s 101* of the *Children Act*

1989 may prescribe other orders (e.g. supervision) and make the necessary modifications to *ss 25* and *26* of the *Children and Young Persons Act 1969* so as to include care orders made under the 1989 Act.

17 Death of Child

17.1 References

Children Act 1989, Sch 2, para 20
Working Together, HMSO 1991
Children's Homes Regulations 1991 (SI 1991 No 1506) Reg 19(2)(a)

17.2 DEFINITIONS

The responsible authority for a children's home is the local authority if a community home, the managers of a controlled or assisted community home, voluntary organisation providing the home and the person carrying on a registered children's home.

17.3 SUMMARY OF POWERS AND DUTIES

In the event of the death of a child being looked after by a local authority, the local authority must

(a) notify the Secretary of State

(b) notify parents or non-parents with parental responsibility.

The local authority may, in the case of a child 'looked after' by a local authority,

(a) arrange burial or cremation

(b) pay expenses [*CA Sch 2, para 20*].

If a child dies in a voluntary or registered children's home, the responsible authority must

(a) notify the Secretary of State

(b) notify parents and non-parents with parental responsibility

(c) notify any person paying fees and expenses at the home

(d) notify the District Health Authority.

17.4 *Schedule 2* of the *CA 89* applies to children being looked after by a local authority (i.e. accommodated or in care). Notification to the Secretary of State will enable consideration of any inquiry under *s 7C* of the *Local Authority Social Services Act 1970* that may be thought necessary. It would also of course be a matter for report to the Social Services Committee. Reference to the Area Child Protection Committee will be necessary where child abuse is confirmed or suspected (see DOH guidance *Working Together*). In such cases separate notification to the DOH is required.

17.5 Notice of the death must give all the details known to the responsible authority.

17.6 The *Children's Homes Regulations* apply to all homes, but where the local authority is the 'responsible authority' notification of death is required only under the Schedule to the 1989 Act. The regulations also require notice of serious harm to be given to the Secretary of State and parents etc.

17.7 **Discretionary powers**

Where a child is being looked after by a local authority the consent of every person with parental responsibility should be obtained (so far as reasonably practicable) before the authority arranges for burial or cremation. Cremation is not permissible if it is not in accordance with the child's religious persuasion.

17.8 Payment of expenses in attending the funeral of any person with parental responsibility, relative, friend, or other person connected with the child may be made if it appears that the person could not otherwise attend without undue financial hardship and the circumstances warrant such payment. The local authority may recover the cost of burial or cremation arranged by them for a child under 16.

18 Delay

18.1 **References**

Children Act 1989, ss 8, 10, 11, 32, 93 and *Sch 11, paras 1(3), 2* and *3(1)*
The Family Proceedings Rules 1991 (SI 1991 No 1247)
The Family Proceedings Courts (Children Act 1989) Rules 1991 (SI 1991 No 1395)
The Children (Allocation of Proceedings) Order 1991 (SI 1991 No 1677)
Department of Health guidance

18.2 **PROCEDURES TO AVOID DELAY**

Courts are charged with the duty of ensuring that certain cases are dealt with speedily by drawing up timetables for the hearings [*ss 11* and *32*]. The Act also provides other means of avoiding delay through transfer of proceedings from one court to another and, for example, by enabling emergency protection orders to be made by a single justice. There are also provisions regarding jurisdiction, procedure, evidence and written statement of case.

18.3 **Family proceedings**

In proceedings for a *s 8* order, or proceedings in which the question of making one arises, or any other question with respect to one, (for example variation/discharge), the Act requires the court to draw up a timetable to determine the question without delay. The *s 8* order may be made in any family proceedings as defined in *s 10* (see FAMILY PROCEEDINGS (22)), whether on the court's own motion or on application by persons entitled or given leave to apply (see SECTION 8 ORDERS (41)). Once the issue has arisen and from the start of a free-standing application for such an order, the court is bound to draw up a timetable in accordance with court rules [*s 11*].

18.4 **Care and supervision orders**

The court hearing an application for a care order, supervision order or education supervision order is similarly under a duty to draw up a timetable to dispose of the application without delay. In addition, timetabling is required when hearing an application for any other order under *Part IV* of the Act, i.e. orders varying or discharging care, supervision orders, orders for contact and interim orders [*s 32*].

18.5 **Court rules**

Statutory Instruments 1247 and *1395* specify the periods within which certain steps must be taken and provide for a GAL, for example, to advise on the appropriate timing of the proceedings or any part of them.

18.6 **JURISDICTION AND PROCEDURE**

Commencement and transfer of proceedings *Sch 11* and *SI 1991 No 1677* make provision for the transfer of proceedings or parts of proceedings between courts

Delay 18.6

at any stage. These provisions, together with the procedural rules regarding preliminary hearings, are all capable of speeding up the resolution of issues involving the welfare of children.

19 Duration of Orders and their Effect

19.1 **References**

Children Act 1989, ss 9 and *91*

19.2 As a general rule all orders under the Act cease to have effect when the child concerned reaches the age of 18. Orders for maintenance may specify a later age.

19.3 *Section 8* orders cease to have effect when the child reaches the age of 16, and should not normally be made to last beyond that age unless the court has found exceptional circumstances and extends the duration of the order. Even then it must cease when the child has reached the age of 18 [*ss 9(6)* and *(7)* and *91(10)* and *(11)*].

19.4 The making of a care order will discharge any *s 8* order, any supervision order (supervision or interim supervision order under *s 31(1)(b)* and *s 38*), wardship, and any school attendance order [*s 91(2), (3), (4)* and *(5)*].

19.5 The making of a residence order in respect of a child subject to a care order discharges the care order [*s 91(1)*].

19.6 Where an application for a contact order under *s 34* has been refused, no further application may be made within six months without leave of the court [*s 91(17)*].

19.7 On disposing of an application under the 1989 Act the court may order that no further application for any specified order shall be made without leave of the court [*s 91(14)*].

19.8 No further application may be made within six months of:

(*a*) the discharge of a care or supervision or education supervision order,

(*b*) the substitution of a supervision order for a care order, or

(*c*) an application for a child assessment order

without the leave of the court. (These restrictions do not apply to interim orders) [*s 91(15)*].

20 Emergency Protection of Children

20.1 References

Children Act 1989, ss 37, 43-51, 102 and Sch 3, Part 1
Police and Criminal Evidence Act 1984
Child Abduction Act 1984
Legal Aid Act 1988
Department of Health guidance Vol 1
The Family Proceedings Rules 1991 (SI 1991 No 1247)
The Family Proceedings Courts (Children Act 1989) Rules 1991 (SI 1991 No 1395)
The Refuges (Children's Homes and Foster Placements) Regulations 1991 (SI 1991 No 1507)
The Emergency Protection Order (Transfer of Responsibilities) Regulations 1991 (SI 1991 No 1414)
Working Together HMSO 1991
Report of the Inquiry into Child Abuse in Cleveland, Cm 412 HMSO 1988

20.2 BACKGROUND

The *Children Act 1989* provides a number of measures for the short-term protection of children. A new 'child assessment order' has been introduced, the former 'place of safety' order has been replaced by the 'emergency protection order' and police powers have been revised. Powers relating to search and entry, disclosure of a child's whereabouts, and abduction and recovery of children are all contained within the Act itself which repeals previous legislation except for police powers in cases of danger to life and limb.

20.3 PRIOR INVESTIGATION

The need to consider emergency action will arise from the investigations carried out, e.g. by a local authority having reasonable cause to suspect that the child is suffering or is likely to suffer significant harm. The local authority's duty to investigate is set out in *s 47*. This duty requires them 'to decide whether they should take any action to safeguard or promote the child's welfare'. The investigation may conclude that no action is required, because alternative ways have been found to achieve an assessment, or an alleged abuser has agreed to leave the child's home. Further, the action required is not necessarily an application to the court for an order as local authority inquiries should be directed towards establishing whether to make application to the court 'or exercise any of their other powers under this Act with respect to the child'. This allows the local authority to consider what family support services could be made available. (The local authority is also under a duty to apply for a child assessment order (or emergency protection order, care order, or supervision order) if refused access to, or information on, the whereabouts of the child concerned [*s 47(6)*].)

Under *s 37* a court hearing family proceedings may direct a local authority to investigate and consideration must be given to what action, if any, should be taken.

20.4 Emergency Protection of Children

20.4 GENERAL PRINCIPLES

Applications for a child assessment order or emergency protection order are not 'family proceedings' as defined in *CA 89, s 8(3)*. Courts must therefore either make or refuse to make the order applied for and cannot make other orders on its own motion. There is one exception to this rule in *s 43*, where a court hearing an application for a child assessment order may make an emergency protection order if satisfied there are grounds for doing so. The court must be satisfied that making the order would be better for the child than making no order at all and the court must make the child's welfare its paramount consideration [see *CA 89 s 1*].

20.5 SUMMARY OF PROVISIONS

The Table below sets out the provisions for assessment, protection orders, and police powers in summary form.

Ways to secure assessment and emergency protection

	Child Assessment Order s 43	*Emergency Protection Order s 44*	*Police Protection s 46*
Who applies:	Local authority or NSPCC [*s 43(1)*]	Any person on grounds (a). Local authority or NSPCC on (b) or (c)	A constable [*s 46(1)*]
To whom:	Magistrates (or court which ordered investigation under *s 37(1)*) or where proceedings are pending.	Magistrates (or court which ordered investigation under *s 37(1)*) or where proceedings are pending.	Not applicable.
Grounds:	(*a*) the applicant has reasonable cause to suspect that the child is suffering, or is likely to suffer significant harm; (*b*) an assessment is needed to find out whether the child is suffering or likely to suffer significant harm; (*c*) it is unlikely that an assessment will be made or be satisfactory without an order [*s 43(1)*].	(*a*) the court must be satisfied that there is reasonable cause to believe that a child is likely to suffer significant harm if not removed to safe accommodation or does not remain in such a place; (*b*) if LA is applying, that they are already investigating under *s 47(1)(b)* and that access to child is being frustrated and there is reasonable cause to believe access is required urgently. (*c*) similar to (*b*) for NSPCC [*s 44(1)*].	Reasonable cause to believe that a child is likely to suffer significant harm unless child kept or moved to suitable accommodation [*s 46(1)*].

Emergency Protection of Children 20.5

	Child Assessment Order s 43	Emergency Protection Order s 44	Police Protection s 46
Can court make another order:	Yes if there are grounds for an EPO and if court believes it ought to make such an order [s 43(3) and (4)].	No. It is either an EPO or no order.	Not applicable.
How long:	Assessment for up to 7 days from date court specifies it should start [s 43(5)].	Up to 8 days (or longer if final day is Sunday or bank holiday). Successful applicant can apply for one extension for up to 7 further days. But applicant shall return child if it is safe to do so [s 44(10) and s 45].	72 hours [s 46(6)].
Powers:	Applicant to arrange assessment as specified in order [s 43(7)].	To put child in safe accommodation or keep in such. To arrange medical, psychiatric or other assessment specified in order [s 44(4)(b) and s 44(6)–(9)].	To put child in safe place, or to make sure child is not removed from such a place.
Duties:	Those in position to produce child (usually parents) to such person named in order and any other specifications in order [s 43(6)].	Person who has power to do so must produce child to applicant [s 44(4)(a)].	Police to inform LA, child, find out child's wishes and feelings, parents, and other persons with parental responsibility, any person with whom the child living before s/he was taken into police protection [s 46(3) and (4)].
Parental responsibility:	Stays with those who have it at time of order.	Gives it to applicant but limited [s 44(4)(c) and (5)(b)].	Police do not acquire PR.
Rights of child:	If the child is of sufficient understanding then s/he may refuse to submit to medical, psychiatric examination or other assessment [s 43(8)].	If the child is of sufficient understanding then may refuse to submit to medical, psychiatric examination or other assessment [s 44(7)].	Inform child why PP is being used. Find out child's wishes and feelings [s 46(3)(c) and (d)].
Can child be removed from home:	Only if order specifies and if removal relates to assessment [s 43(9)].	Yes [s 44(4)(b)].	Yes.

20.5 Emergency Protection of Children

	Child Assessment Order s 43	*Emergency Protection Order s 44*	*Police Protection s 46*
Contact:	Order must specify contact with other persons as court thinks fit if order specifies removal [s 43(10)].	May give directions on contact which is or is not allowed between child and named persons but subject to directions allow reasonable contact with: — parents — non-parents with parental responsibility — any person with whom child living immediately before order — anyone with rights to contact — any person acting on behalf of above [s 44(13)].	The designated officer shall allow contact with the following, as is reasonable and in the child's best interests: — child's parents — non-parents with parental responsibility — any person with whom child living immediately before PP — anyone in whose favour a contact order exists — any person acting on behalf of the above [s 46(10)].
Notice/ inform:	Applicant as far as is reasonably practical to ensure notice to: — those providing accommodation for child — child's parents — non-parents with parental responsibility — any other person caring for child — any person with contact or allowed contact under a s 34 contact order — the child — any person providing a 'refuge' [s 43(11)].	May be *ex parte* otherwise notice to: — LA providing accommodation, — persons caring for the child — any person providing a 'refuge'.	Inform: — LA where child is and where child normally is, if different — parents — non-parents with parental responsibility — any other person with whom child was living immediately before PP [s 46(3)(a) and (4)].
Variation of order during its currency:	Yes [s 43(12)].	Directions on contact and medical or psychiatric examination or treatment may be varied by the court.	Not applicable.
Return home:	Yes. But only applicable if court has ordered removal for assessment.	Yes. If applicant believes it safe for child then 'he shall return the child'. But applicant can reactivate powers after return without going back to court [s 44(10)].	Not applicable.

56

Emergency Protection of Children 20.6

	Child Assessment Order s 43	*Emergency Protection Order s 44*	*Police Protection s 46*
Appeal:	Yes [s 94].	Yes. After 72 hours. But not if person was present at hearing and not in respect of an extension of EPO [s 45(8) and (11)].	No.
Who may appeal:	Parties to the proceedings.	— child — parent — any person with parental responsibility — any person with whom child living immediately before EPO made [s 45(8) and (11)].	Not applicable.

Powers of discovery and entry

1. Emergency protection order and

    (i) direction to disclose — *s 48(1)*

    (ii) enter and search (no force) — *s 48(3)*

    (iii) warrant (reasonable force) if refused entry or access likely to be refused — *s 48(9)*

    N.B. offence of obstruction to entry and search — *s 48(7)*
    offence of obstruction or removal or retention of child under EPO — *s 44(15)*
    offence of abduction of child in care/subject of EPO/in police protection — *s 49*

2. Section 17(1)(e) of the *Police and Criminal Evidence Act 1984*

3. Search warrant for:
    child under supervision order
    protected child under adoption legislation
    inspection of certain homes and premises — *s 102*

4. Authority to search and enter for child in care/subject to EPO/ in police protection — *s 50(3)*

5. Order to disclose/produce child abducted — *s 50(3)*

20.6 CHILD ASSESSMENT ORDER

This order enables an assessment of the child to be made where the court is satisfied that the applicant has reasonable cause to suspect that s/he is suffering or likely to suffer significant harm, (presumably the definitions of 'harm' and 'significant' in *s 31(9)* and *(10)* apply). Where access to a child is required as a matter of urgency, the appropriate application would be for an emergency protection order, although the court may grant an emergency protection order even though a child assessment order has been applied for.

20.7 Emergency Protection of Children

In contrast to the grounds for an emergency protection order, i.e. 'reasonable grounds to believe', which connote confidence in the material put forward, the grounds for a child assessment order i.e. 'reasonable cause to suspect' imply slight or even no evidence. Efforts to obtain an assessment by agreement should be documented so that the court can be satisfied, as it must, that without an order it is unlikely that an assessment will be made. This condition in *s 43(1)* highlights yet again the emphasis in the Act on co-operation between parents and the local authority, and the need to exhaust 'non-coercive' measures.

20.7 **Procedure**

The requirement for notice of the application (see 20.5 SUMMARY OF PROVISIONS) and therefore a full hearing detracts from the notion of urgency, although the order is still intended to meet serious concerns for a child. Rules of Court provide for variation and discharge of the order by the applicant and those persons referred to in *s 43(11)*. The rules specify who must be given notice of the application [*SI 1991 No 1395 r 2(3)* and *Sch 2; SI 1991 No 1247 r 4(2)* and *App 3*]. The nature of the hearing and the seven-day time limit for assessments to be completed (see 20.5 SUMMARY OF PROVISIONS) will require considerable preparation beforehand, possibly by multi-disciplinary conference. Appeal against the making or refusal of a child assessment order will lie to the High Court [*s 94(1)*] and the Court in disposing of an application may limit further applications by specified persons or within the following six months without leave [*s 91(15)*].

20.8 **Court's powers and duties**

The effect of the order is a requirement on 'any person who is in a position to produce the child

(*a*)   to produce her/him to such person as may be named in the order; and

(*b*)   to comply with such directions relating to the assessment of the child as the court thinks fit to specify in the order'.

The order also authorises any person carrying out the assessment to do so in accordance with the terms of the order.

20.9   A child 'of sufficient understanding to make an informed decision' may nevertheless refuse to submit to a medical or psychiatric examination or other assessment. A guardian *ad litem*, if appointed, must help the court determine whether a child can exercise this right and also advise the child [*SI 1991 No 1395, r 11(4)* and *SI 1991 No 1247, r 4(11)*]. This limiting of the effect of the court's orders is repeated throughout the Act, (see 5.13 CHILD'S UNDERSTANDING AND LEGAL REPRESENTATION) and gives substance to the notion of children's rights.

20.10 The court may direct that the child be kept away from home for a period or periods, but only if it is necessary for the purposes of the assessment. Absence from home (the cause of much concern in the more recent public enquiries) is not to be taken as a measure of protection for the child but as a means of achieving an adequate assessment. If directions are given for keeping the child away from home the court must also give directions as to contact the child is to be allowed to have with 'other persons'. Contact is not restricted therefore to those with parental responsibility. The importance of contacts with a broad range of adults and other children is a feature of the Act. Correspondingly there is an onus on local authorities to be fully prepared to meet requests for contact. This will involve guidance and support for the 'carers' and also the presentation of any evidence of unsuitability of the proposed contacts.

Emergency Protection of Children 20.16

20.11 **Guardians ad litem**

The Court must appoint a GAL for the child unless satisfied that it is not necessary to do so in order to safeguard her/his interests [*s 41*] (see GUARDIANS (24)).

20.12 **Legal aid**

Civil legal aid may be granted in all proceedings under the *Children Act 1989*. The means and merit tests are waived for these proceedings (see LEGAL AID (27)).

20.13 **Refusal to comply**

No criminal offence arises merely from a failure to produce a child in compliance with the order. If the failure causes sufficient concern, powers to take into police protection might be exercised (see 20.5 SUMMARY OF PROVISIONS). Unlike the emergency protection order there is no provision for an order to disclose whereabouts, no provision for entry and search warrants, and no offence of obstruction. Circumstances may however exist which would justify application for an emergency protection order. Such an application may be heard *ex parte* under the rules, therefore avoiding delay in obtaining an order.

20.14 **EMERGENCY PROTECTION ORDER**

This order enables a child to be removed from or to be kept where s/he is. Under *s 47(6)* a local authority carrying out enquiries must apply for an emergency protection or other order if refused access to the child in question or denied information as to her/his whereabouts. This provision reflects the concerns raised at a number of public inquiries in recent years. There was some doubt under previous legislation whether the authority of a Magistrate's order could, for example, authorise the retention of a child in hospital. The legislation is now framed so as to remove such doubts and also to ensure that local authorities take steps to see a child who is the subject of enquiries [*s 47(4)*]. The order may be made for no more than eight days, and where the local authority or NSPCC were the original applicant they may apply for one extension only of no more than seven days.

20.15 **Procedure**

Rules of Court permit both *ex parte* and *inter partes* hearings, although it is probable that *inter partes* hearings will be confined mainly to applications to discharge. Application may be made by any person as was the case in previous legislation. If the applicant was not the local authority, Rules of Court require a copy of the order to be served on the local authority [*SI 1991 No 1395, r 21(8)*]. That in turn may trigger the local authority duty to investigate under *s 47*. The *Emergency Protection Order (Transfer of Responsibilities) Regulations 1991 (SI 1991 No 1414)* makes provision for transfer of an order obtained by another person to the local authority. A single justice may hear applications *ex parte* [*SI 1991 No 1395, r 2(5)*].

20.16 **Grounds for the order**

The grounds in *s 44(1)(b)* and *(c)* are complementary to the provisions of *s 47(6)*, (refusal of access or information as to the whereabouts of the child concerned). Department of Health guidance emphasises the necessity to prove all elements of *s 44(1)(b)* and *(c)* i.e.:

20.17 Emergency Protection of Children

- reasonable cause to suspect significant harm in the first place
- enquiries already being undertaken
- access to the child has been refused
- refusal is frustrating the enquiry
- refusal is unreasonable
- access is required as a matter of urgency.

The Act imposes a heavy burden on the applicant and gives the court some discretion in considering what is a reasonable request for access. It may be prudent to inform the person who is thought able to produce the child of the consequences of the refusal. Although Department of Health guidance suggests there is no justification for failing to act because of lack of information occasioned by inability to see the child, it is still necessary to show reasonable cause to suspect significant harm (the basis of enquiries having been started under *s 47(1)(b)*). The courts may not be prepared to infer that from the refusal of access alone. Consequently there may still be difficulty in determining appropriate action. However, especially in the case of young children, not at school, who have not been seen for some time the consequences of failure to see such children who are the subject of undeveloped concerns may fairly be said to give rise to suspicion of significant harm; an easier burden to discharge than belief that significant harm has been caused.

The grounds in *s 44(1)(a)* will apply if there is reasonable cause to believe that a child is likely to suffer significant harm – a prospective test which may be satisfied by evidence of past events in relation to a particular child or other family members.

20.17 Evidence

Most, if not all, exclusionary rules of evidence will not apply to applications for an emergency protection order as the court is empowered by *s 45(7)* to take account of any statement in any report presented 'in the course of or in connection with the hearing' or any evidence given relevant to the application. Thus, hearsay evidence which is often highly relevant, though normally legally inadmissible to prove the truth of statements, may now be presented.

Notice of the making or extension of an order or application to discharge must be served by the court on parties to the proceedings and any person with whom the child is living. If the order was made *ex parte* the order must also be served within 48 hours on the local authority [*SI 1991 No 1395, r 21(7)(8)* and *Sch 2*].

20.18 Effect of the order

The order applies as a direction to any person in a position to do so to comply with any request by the applicant to produce the child; it authorises removal of the child to accommodation provided by the applicant and being kept there, or prevention of the child's removal from where s/he was accommodated immediately before the making of the order. The order also gives the applicant parental responsibility for the child [see *CA 89 s 44(4)(c)*]. Under *s 91(6)* a care order has effect 'subject to an emergency protection order'.

If it is thought necessary to enter and search premises to remove the child, specific authority to do so should be sought (see 20.32 ENTER AND SEARCH (NO

FORCE) below). The power given to remove or prevent removal of the child is only to be exercised in order to safeguard the welfare of the child [s 44(5)(a)]. Parental responsibility granted to the applicant is limited to action reasonably required to safeguard or promote the welfare of the child during the currency of the order [s 44(5)(b)].

20.19 **'Cleveland Inquiry' guidelines**

The report of the Inquiry (Cm 412 HMSO 1988) cautions against orders for longer than absolutely necessary, and orders executed late at night. There has since been other criticism of 'place of safety orders' and the care and caution to be taken is now referred to in *Working Together*.

20.20 **Return of the child**

Safeguards to retain contact with the family are introduced in *s 44(10)* which places the applicant under a duty to return or allow a child to be removed when it appears safe for the child. (Regard should be had to the provisions of *Sch 2, para 5* allowing, for example, a suspected adult abuser to be accommodated by a local authority away from the child's home.) The child will have to be returned to the care of the person from whose care s/he is removed, or, if not reasonably practicable, to parents or persons with parental responsibility or such other person as the applicant (with the agreement of the court) considers appropriate [s 44(11)]. However, powers to remove may again be exercised during the currency of the order if it appears (to the applicant) that a change in the circumstances of the case make it necessary to do so. Discretion therefore lies with the applicant although the strict time limits i.e. eight days and one extension only of seven days, would not normally permit much movement or allow for challenge.

20.21 **Contact**

Subject to any direction of the court (see below) the applicant must allow reasonable contact with a broad range of persons (see Table 20.5). Practical difficulties in arranging contact do not absolve the applicant from allowing contact. What is reasonable may differ depending upon the accommodation provided – hospital, community home or foster home – and the numbers seeking contact with the child. Where difficulty is anticipated, directions from the court should be sought.

20.22 **The court's powers and duties**

The court may give and vary directions as to (*a*) contact and (*b*) medical and psychiatric examination or other assessments at any time during the currency of the order [s 44(6)(9)]. As with a child assessment order a child of sufficient understanding to make an informed decision may refuse to submit to examination or assessment (a GAL may advise the court on this). The court may impose conditions in any direction and, for example, limit or otherwise define contact and in particular rule out any examination or assessment unless otherwise directed by the court [s 44(8)]. Under *SI 1991 No 1395, r 18* leave of the court is required before the child can be medically or psychiatrically examined or otherwise assessed for the purposes of preparing expert evidence for use in the proceedings. The court may give additional directions to assist discovery of children's whereabouts.

20.23 Emergency Protection of Children

20.23 Discharge of order

The persons entitled to apply for discharge of the order are set out in the Table in 20.5 above. No application may be made until 72 hours after the making of the order. Where a person otherwise entitled had been given notice of the original hearing and attended, they are barred from applying [*s 45(11)*]. If an emergency protection order has been extended no application for discharge may then be heard. The exclusion is presumably justified by the requirement that a court may only extend an emergency protection order if satisfied that it has reasonable cause to believe that the child is likely to suffer significant harm if the order is not extended.

20.24 Appeal

The right to apply for discharge is the effective appeal against the making of an order. Given the short duration of the order a right of appeal as such would not be practicable, and accordingly *s 45(10)* excludes from the general principle in *s 94* that an appeal lies against the making or refusal of an order under the Act by a magistrates court. No appeal may be made against the making of or refusal to make an emergency protection order or against any direction given in connection with that order.

20.25 Offences

The Act creates an offence of intentional obstruction of persons exercising the power to remove or prevent the removal of a child, where an emergency protection order is in force. (See also offences of obstruction under *s 48(7)* at 20.34 OBSTRUCTION.)

20.26 POLICE PROTECTION

The provisions of *s 46* replace previous legislation allowing a child to be detained by police for up to eight days. A child may now be taken into police protection for no more than seventy-two hours where a constable has reasonable cause to believe that s/he would otherwise be likely to suffer significant harm [*CA 89 s 46(6)*]. The constable may remove the child to suitable accommodation or prevent removal from where s/he is being accommodated.

20.27 Notice

The constable taking a child into police protection has the specified duties set out in *s 46(3)* and *(4)* below.

'*(3)* As soon as is reasonably practicable after taking a child into police protection, the constable concerned shall

(*a*) inform the local authority within whose area the child was found of the steps that have been, and are proposed to be, taken with respect to the child under this section and the reasons for taking them;

(*b*) give details to the authority within whose area the child is ordinarily resident ('the appropriate authority') of the place at which the child is being accommodated;

(c) inform the child (if s/he appears capable of understanding)

    (i) of the steps that have been taken with respect to her/him under this section and of the reasons for taking them; and

    (ii) of the further steps that may be taken with respect to her/him under this section;

(d) take such steps as are reasonably practicable to discover the wishes and feelings of the child;

(e) secure that the case is inquired into by an officer designated for the purposes of this section by the chief officer of the police area concerned; and

(f) where the child was taken into police protection by being removed to accommodation which is not provided

    (i) by or on behalf of a local authority; or

    (ii) as a refuge, in compliance with the requirements of section 51, secure that he is moved to accommodation which is so provided.

(4) As soon as is reasonably practicable after taking a child into police protection, the constable concerned shall take such steps as are reasonably practicable to inform –

(a) the child's parents;

(b) every person who is not a parent of his but who has parental responsibility for her/him; and

(c) any other person with whom the child was living immediately before being taken into police protection,

of the steps that he has taken under this section with respect to the child, the reasons for taking them and the further steps that may be taken with respect to her/him under this section.'

The designated officer referred to in *s 46(3)(e)* must release the child after completion of enquiries unless s/he considers that there is still reasonable cause to believe that the child would be likely to suffer significant harm if released.

20.28 Designated police officer

S/he may apply to the court for an emergency protection order on behalf of the local authority whether or not the authority know or agree to it being made. Given the constable's duty to inform and, in certain circumstances, place in local authority accommodation, there will normally be close liaison and the authority may well ask the officer to exercise this power. The formal liaison provisions of *s 47(11)* (see 11.17 CHILD PROTECTION) somewhat surprisingly do not apply to the police, but co-operation is stressed in, for example, *Working Together* the Department of Health guidance on inter-agency co-operation for the protection of children from abuse. Similar guidance may be issued by the Secretary of State under *s 7* of the *Local Authority Social Services Act 1970*. Neither the constable taking into police protection nor the designated officer acquire parental responsibility for the child. The latter 'shall do what is reasonable in all the circumstances of the case for the purpose of safeguarding or promoting the child's welfare (having regard in particular to the length of the period during which the child will be so protected)' [*s 46(9)*].

20.29 Emergency Protection of Children

20.29 Contact

The designated officer or local authority, if the child is placed in local authority accommodation, must allow a range of persons (see Table in 20.5) such contact, if any, with the child as is both reasonable and in the child's best interests. A child accommodated for more than 24 hours under any provision of the Act falls within the definition in *s 22* of a child 'looked after' by a local authority. It follows therefore that the duty to consult the child (and others) regarding contact [*s 22(4)* and *(5)*] and to promote and maintain contact with the child's family [*Sch 2 para 15*] apply where the police place the child in local authority accommodation.

20.30 Discovery and entry

The making of an emergency protection order allows the court, in addition to making provision to assist in the discovery of children whose whereabouts are unknown, to authorise entry and search of specified premises [*s 48*].

20.31 Direction to disclose

If the applicant for an emergency protection order does not have adequate information as to the child's whereabouts, the court may order any other person to whom that information is available to disclose any information s/he may have. The defence of self-incrimination or that of her/his spouse is not available if such an order is made, but any statement or admission made in complying with the order is not admissible in any proceedings for an offence other than perjury [*s 48(1)* and *(2)*].

20.32 Enter and search (no force)

An emergency protection order may also authorise the applicant to enter specified premises and search for the child concerned. Authorisation under *s 48(3)* does not allow the use of force. The order may also cover search for another child on the specified premises, if the court is satisfied that there is reasonable cause to believe an emergency protection order ought to be made in respect of that child. If such a child is then found and the applicant is satisfied that the grounds for an order exist in respect of her/him the order has effect as if it were an emergency protection order dating from the making of the order authorising the search for that child [*s 48(4)* and *(5)*]. The applicant must inform the court of the result of the search for the other child.

20.33 Warrant – reasonable force

If any person attempting to exercise powers under an emergency protection order has been prevented from doing so by being refused entry to the premises concerned, or if access to the child concerned was likely to be so prevented, application may be made for a warrant authorising any constable to assist in gaining entry or access using reasonable force if necessary [*s 48(9)*]. The court must be satisfied that the applicant has been prevented from exercising powers under an emergency protection order and this may refer specifically to the power to enter and search rather than the general authority to remove. To avoid any doubt care should be taken to seek an order under *s 48(3)* if there is evidence that access to the child may be refused. The applicant may accompany the constable executing a warrant unless the court orders otherwise and the court may direct that a doctor, nurse or health visitor may accompany the constable.

20.34 Obstruction

It is a criminal offence to intentionally obstruct any person exercising the power of entry and search under *s 48(3)* and *(4)* [*s 48(7)*].

20.35 Police and Criminal Evidence Act 1984, s 17(1)

'17(1) Subject to the following provisions of this section, and without prejudice to any other enactment, a constable may enter and search any premises for the purpose

(*a*) of executing

   (i) a warrant of arrest issued in connection with or arising out of criminal proceedings; or

   (ii) a warrant of commitment issued under section 76 of the Magistrates' Courts Act 1980;

(*b*) of arresting a person for an arrestable offence;

(*c*) of arresting a person for an offence under

   (i) section 1 (prohibition of uniforms in connection with political objects), 4 (prohibition of offensive weapons at public meetings and processions), or 5 (prohibition of offensive conduct conducive to breaches of the peace) of the Public Order Act 1936;

   (ii) any enactment contained in sections 6 to 8 or 10 of the Criminal Law Act 1977 (offences relating to entering and remaining on property);

(*d*) of recapturing a person who is unlawfully at large and whom he is pursuing; or

(*e*) of saving life or limb or preventing serious damage to property.

(2) Except for the purpose specified in paragraph (e) of subsection (1) above, the powers of entry and search conferred by this section–

(*a*) are only exercisable if the constable has reasonable grounds for believing that the person whom he is seeking is on the premises; and

(*b*) are limited, in relation to premises consisting of two or more separate dwellings, to powers to enter and search

   (i) any parts of the premises which the occupiers of any dwelling comprised in the premises use in common with the occupiers of any other such dwelling, and

   (ii) any such dwelling in which the constable has reasonable grounds for believing the person whom he is seeking may be.

(3) The powers of entry and search conferred by this section are only exercisable for the purposes specified in subsection (1)(c)(ii) above by a constable in uniform.

(4) The power of search conferred by this section is only a power to search to the extent that is reasonably required for the purpose for which the power of entry is exercised.

(5) Subject to subsection (6) below, all the rules of common law under which a constable has power to enter premises without a warrant are hereby abolished.

20.36 Emergency Protection of Children

(6) Nothing in subsection (5) above affects any power of entry to deal with or prevent a breach of the peace.'

20.36 **Other search warrants** *(Children Act 1989, s 102)*

Where a child is *(a)* subject to a supervision order, *(b)* a protected child under adoption legislation, or *(c)* is accommodated in certain homes or premises and access to the child or entry to the premises has been refused or is likely to be prevented, the court may issue a warrant authorising a constable to assist using reasonable force if necessary. The specific rights of access which, if frustrated, give grounds to apply for a warrant are set out in *s 102(6)*.

20.37 **ABDUCTION AND RECOVERY OF CHILDREN IN CARE**

Abduction

Sections 49 and *50* of the Act apply to children which are the subject of

(a)   a care order,

(b)   an emergency protection order, or

(c)   in police protection.

Section 49 creates an offence if any person knowingly and without lawful authority or reasonable excuse,

  (i)   takes the child away from the responsible person;

  (ii) keeps such a child from the responsible person; or

  (iii) induces, assists or incites such a child to run away or stay away from the responsible person.

'Responsible person' means any person who for the time being has care of a child by virtue of *(a)*, *(b)* or *(c)* above.

20.38 Abduction of children from other forms of lawful control (of parents etc.) is dealt with under *s 2* of the *Child Abduction Act 1984*, *s 18* of the *Child Abduction and Custody Act 1985*, and *s 32* of the *Children and Young Persons Act 1969* (children under supervision and taken to a place of safety etc.).

20.39 **Recovery of abducted children**

A court may make a recovery order in respect of children to whom *s 49* applies (as set out above in 20.37) or who have been abducted or run away, directing any person in a position to do so to produce the child to an authorised person or disclose information as to the child's whereabouts to a constable or officer of the court and authorising removal of the child and entry and search for the child using reasonable force if necessary [*s 50(3)*].

20.40 The local authority or other person having parental responsibility, or in the case of police protection, the designated officer may apply for a recovery order. Intentional obstruction of recovery is an offence. As with other provisions no excuse of self-incrimination or incrimination of a spouse is allowed, but statements or admissions in complying with an order will not be admissible in proceedings for an offence other than perjury.

20.41 REFUGES

A local authority or voluntary organisation may provide either in a voluntary or registered home or in a foster home a refuge for children who appear to be at risk or harm. *The Refuges (Children's Homes and Foster Placements) Regulations 1991 (SI 1991 No 1507)* sets out the requirements for certification, which exempts the home from the provisions relating to offences of abduction and harbouring under the *Children Act 1989* and other legislation. Police may place a child in police protection in a refuge if removed from accommodation other than that which was provided by or on behalf of the local authority. Authority to search for children abducted from care is provided in *s 50(3)* (see 1.4).

21 Family Assistance Orders

21.1 References

Children Act 1989, s 16

21.2 MAKING THE ORDER

Family assistance orders can be made in family proceedings (see FAMILY PROCEEDINGS (22)) where the court is satisfied that the circumstances of the case are exceptional and that everyone (other than the child) who is to be named in the order consents.

Family assistance orders aim to provide short-term help for families in difficulties. They cannot last for more than six months [*s 16(5)*].

The order itself will require that a probation officer or officer from a local authority be available to advise, assist and where appropriate befriend anyone named in the order [*s 16(1)*].

Those who can be named in the order are any parent or guardian of the child, any person with whom the child is living or in whose favour a contact order is enforced in relation to the child, or the child.

If a *s 8* order (see SECTION 8 ORDERS (41)) is in force when a family assistance order is in force the officer can refer to the court the question of whether the order should be varied or discharged [*s 16(6)*].

A family assistance order can only require a local authority to make one of its officers available if the authority agrees or the child concerned lives or will live in the local authority's area [*s 16(7)*].

22 Family Proceedings

22.1 References
Children Act 1989, ss 8(3) and *10*

22.2 INTRODUCTION

Section 10(1) of the Act gives the court the power to make any *s 8* order in any family proceedings in which a question arises with respect to the welfare of the child. This power exists whether or not anyone has applied for a *s 8* order. It means therefore that the court can make a *s 8* order in family proceedings if it considers the order should be made even though no one has actually asked for it.

22.3 Family proceedings are defined in the Act as being proceedings brought under the following.

— The inherent jurisdiction of the High Court in relation to children; and
— *Parts I, II* and *IV* of the *Children Act 1989*;
— The *Matrimonial Causes Act 1973*;
— The *Domestic Violence and Matrimonial Proceedings Act 1976*;
— The *Adoption Act 1976*;
— The *Domestic Proceedings and Magistrates' Court Act 1978*;
— *Sections 1* and *9* of the *Matrimonial Homes Act 1983*;
— *Part III* of the *Matrimonial Family Proceedings Act 1984*.

[*s 8(3)* and *(4)*].

This means that in any of the proceedings listed above a person can apply for a *s 8* order (although they may need leave to do so) (see SECTION 8 ORDERS (41)). For example, in proceedings for an injunction or order brought under either the *Domestic Violence and Matrimonial Proceedings Act 1976* or the *Domestic Proceedings and Magistrates Court Act 1978*, the parent who is not looking after the child and who may be the subject of an injunction restraining her/him from coming near the home, may apply for a contact order. Even if s/he does not the court could still make one if it thought it was in the child's interests to do so and an order was necessary. This might well affect which court was to hear the proceedings at county court level.

22.4 Another possible impact of this provision is in adoption proceedings or proceedings for an order freeing a child for adoption. In either of those proceedings the court could make a residence order instead of making an adoption order or an order freeing the child for adoption. Hitherto in proceedings for a freeing order, the court has not been able to make a contact order. This no longer applies since in freeing proceedings brought under the *Adoption Act 1976* the court can make a contact order because they are 'family proceedings'.

22.5 Family Proceedings

22.5 DIVORCE, NULLITY AND JUDICIAL SEPARATION

What follows applies equally to proceedings to annul a marriage or to judicial separation proceedings. The Act does not make significant changes to the procedure for obtaining a divorce but it does have a considerable impact on the way in which the position of children is dealt with in divorce proceedings.

Proceedings for divorce are brought under the *Matrimonial Causes Act 1973* and proceedings under that Act are defined as family proceedings [see *CA 89 s 8(4)*]. The court's previous powers to make custody and access orders have been removed and replaced with the power to make *s 8* orders (see SECTION 8 ORDERS (41)).

22.6 In the past when considering the position of children on divorce, the courts have normally made orders for custody, care and control and access even where arrangements have been agreed between the parents. Now, before making any order, the court must consider whether to do so would be better for the child than not making an order and should not make an order unless one is necessary [*s 1(5)*]. This is likely to mean that in most cases the court will not make any orders in respect of children when their parents obtain a divorce. These changes are reflected in a new procedure for dealing with questions concerning children on divorce.

22.7 As before when submitting a petition for divorce the party doing so must complete a form setting out the arrangements being made and to be made for any children of the family. The form of this statement has been changed and it is now a great deal more detailed than before. The form also provides for the other parent to sign it indicating that they are in agreement with the arrangements as set out. This is new.

Before the Act came into force, either or both parents had to attend court and explain to the judge what the arrangements for the children were. Only when this had been done could the judge make a certificate (known as a *s 41* certificate because it is dealt with in *s 41* of the *Matrimonial Causes Act 1973*), stating that the arrangements for the children were satisfactory or as satisfactory as they could be in the circumstances. The divorce could not be finalised until that *s 41* certificate had been made by the judge. It is still necessary to obtain a *s 41* certificate but the procedure is very different.

22.8 Where there are no other applications relating to the children of the family and the Statement of Arrangements form does not reveal anything which might make the court feel an order was required, the district judge may certify that the provisions of *s 41* have been satisfied without the need for either of the parents to attend the court. This is likely to be the position in the majority of cases where the parents have managed, even with difficulty, to agree the arrangements and there are no concerns about the welfare of the children.

Where the district judge is not satisfied with the arrangements, s/he may give one of the following directions:

— that the parties to the divorce or either of them file further evidence dealing with the arrangements for the children specifying what questions should be dealt with in that evidence;

— order a Welfare Report on all or any of the children;

— order that the parties attend before a district judge.

[*Family Proceedings Rules 1991 (SI 1991 No 1247) r 2.39 and 2.40*].

The district judge will then consider the position again, before deciding whether to grant a *s 41* certificate.

22.9 FINANCIAL SUPPORT

The Act [*s 15* and *Sch 1*] contains provisions to replace previous legislation providing for financial orders for the support of children. However the *Child Support Act 1991* which is expected to come into force in April 1993 makes substantial alterations to the arrangements for financial provision for children which lie beyond the scope of this book. For further information about financial provision for children, reference should be made to specific texts.

23 Foster Parents

23.1 References

Children Act 1989, ss 9(1)(3), 23, 63 and *Schs 2* and *7*
Foster Placement (Children) Regulations 1991 (SI 1991 No 910)
Department of Health guidance Vol 3

23.2 LOCAL AUTHORITY FOSTERING SERVICE

A local authority providing accommodation and maintenance for a child they are 'looking after' has a number of placement options set out in *s 23(2)*. The authority may, in particular place with a family, a relative or any other suitable person on such terms as to payment by the authority or otherwise as the authority may determine. Any person with whom a child is so placed is a 'local authority foster parent' unless s/he is a parent, non-parent with parental responsibility or where the child is in care and there was a residence order in force immediately before the care order was made, a person in whose favour the residence order was made. (For private foster parent see PRIVATE FOSTERING (31)).

23.3 Arrangements must be made when recruiting foster parents to have regard to the different racial groups to which children in need belong [*Sch 2 para 11*].

23.4 The Act and regulations prescribe the procedure for approval and review of foster parents, placement agreements, supervision of placements and records of foster parents. The latter include records of refusal to approve which may be of importance if application for approval is subsequently made to other authorities. The regulations apply to placements by the local authority under *s 23(2)(a)* and voluntary organisations under *s 59(1)(a)*. The regulations do not apply to placement for adoption or with parents etc. of a child in care which are covered by the *Placement of Children with Parents etc. Regulations 1991 (SI 1991 No 893)*. If the child is not in care the parent or other person having parental responsibility with whom a child is placed is not treated as a foster parent. Placement cannot be made with a foster parent unless s/he is approved.

23.5 APPROVAL

The local authority (or voluntary organisation) responsible for the placement of a child is the body which approves a foster parent. The law is now framed so that the authority cannot approve a foster parent who is already approved by another authority. The scheme is intended to provide better regulated and more convenient use of foster homes so that approval of a prospective foster parent living in another authority's area can only be given if that area is consulted, their views taken into account and notice of the decision made given to them.

23.6 At least two referees must be interviewed and the particulars in *Sch 1* to the regulations obtained.

23.7 Approval is of the individual as a foster parent (not the household as formerly) although in granting approval the authority must also be satisfied that the foster parents' household is suitable for any child in respect of whom approval is given. The particulars to be supplied under *Sch 1* to the regulations in this respect are 'particulars of other adult members of the household and children of the family wherever living and other children in the household'. The health of other members of the family may be an important consideration in assessing the suitability of the household and it would be wise to seek such information. The guidance makes it clear that no one has a right to be a foster parent and that 'the aim should be to identify all the factors which contribute to a general picture of the applicant, her family and way of life'. The regulations do not limit the information which authorities may reasonably require in achieving this aim; they are a minimum requirement.

23.8 Approval may be general, or in respect of a particular child, or number and age range of children or of placements of any particular kind or in any particular circumstances. Approval may therefore be given for 'emergency' placements of up to three young children.

23.9 Written notice of refusal to approve must be given.

23.10 **Reviews and termination of approval**

Foster parents and the suitability of their households are to be reviewed annually. The review will take into account the foster parents' views and those of any authority who have placed a child within the preceding year or who have a continuing placement. A report of the review has to be prepared and written notice given of the decision and any variation of the terms of approval (e.g. as to numbers and age range). If the authority are not satisfied as to the suitability of the foster parents under review they may terminate the approval. They must give written notice to the foster parent and any authority who have a child placed.

The complaints procedure in *s 26* of *CA 1989* is open to a local authority foster parent who makes representations about the discharge by the authority or any of the functions under *Part III* in relation to the child.

Termination of approval does not meet that criteria as it is not an action in relation to the child. However the guidance suggests the extension of the statutory scheme voluntarily to include complaints made by foster parents on their own behalf. (Other avenues of complaint may be open to a foster parent, see COMPLAINTS AND REPRESENTATIONS (10).)

23.11 The guidance suggests that the annual review should, if possible, be carried out by a social worker with responsibility for the fostering service who may not be the social worker of a child in placement. Care needs to be taken to ensure that there is no overly 'cosy' supervision by 'foster unit' workers anxious to support a scarce resource. There is no requirement to seek the views of the authority's own social workers with children placed – only the views of other authorities who have placed. This is an unfortunate omission in the statutory scheme which can and should be rectified by the authority's own practice guidance.

23.12 **FOSTER CARE AGREEMENTS – REGULATION 3(6) AND SCHEDULE 2**

Where an approving authority approve a person as a foster parent they '. . .shall nevertheless place no child with him unless he enters into a written agreement with them covering the matters in Sch 2'.

23.13 The foster care agreement under *Sch 2* should not be confused with the individual foster placement agreement under *reg 5(6)* which must be entered into for each child placed. As regards the former it should be noted that corporal punishment is

23.14   Foster Parents

ruled out. The authority may need to supplement such a bold statement with guidance on appropriate measures of control and indeed incorporate any relevant council child care policies in the agreement. The regulations are not exhaustive of the reasonable terms that may be included in an agreement. Similarly, guidance will be necessary on what should be regarded as a 'serious occurrence' affecting the child which must be notified to the authority.

The Schedule also requires the agreement to stipulate that the foster parent give written notice forthwith of *inter alia* any other event affecting either her/his capacity to care for any child or the suitability of her/his household. Matters affecting both adult or children members of the houshold should therefore be disclosed but some examples could be given in explanatory material prepared for foster parents and in their training.

Support and training to be given form part of the written agreement and is emphasised in the guidance. Any assistance in meeting legal liabilities e.g. insurance is also to be included.

23.14 **PLACEMENT**

Placement may only be made if this is the most suitable way for a local authority to perform its duty, and placement with the particular foster parent is the most suitable placement having regard to the circumstances. Social workers for the child will need to have sufficient information to enable them to make such decisions. The foster file and review reports should therefore be available and taken into account.

23.15 Placement has to be with foster parents of the same religious persuasion as the child and who will give an undertaking that the child will be brought up in that religious persuasion, where possible. Authorities will already, in recruiting foster parents, have had regard to the different racial groups within their area.

23.16 The authority may place a child, subject to the terms of approval, with foster parents they have themselves approved. Authorities may place a child with foster parents approved by other authorities provided:

(*a*)   the approving authority consent;

(*b*)   any other authority who already have a child placed consent; and

(*c*)   the authority for the area where the foster parent lives (if not the approving authority) are consulted, their views taken into account and are given notice of the placement.

23.17 **Foster placement agreement** – *Reg 5(6)*

Unless an emergency and immediate placement is made, the placing authority and the foster parent must first enter into a written agreement. The intention is to provide *inter alia* the information necessary for the care of the child and provision of payments, and set out the arrangements for visits and contact with parents etc.

23.18 **Supervision of placements**

Irrespective of the intended duration of the placement, visits to the child in the home must be made at the foster parent's (reasonable) request and, in the first year, at least within one week, then at six-weekly intervals and subsequently at three-monthly intervals. In the case of emergency and immediate placements the visits are to be at least weekly.

23.19 At each visit arrangements must be made, if it is thought appropriate, to see the child alone. Written reports of each visit are to be made. Although such reports are not required to be included in the foster parent file it would be good practice to include them and ensure effective communication between children's social workers and foster unit workers.

23.20 **Termination of placements**

The placing authority must terminate a placement if it no longer appears the most suitable way of performing their duties. The authority acting for the area where a foster parent lives must remove a child as soon as it appears that continuation would be detrimental to the child's welfare. They must then notify the placing authority. The regulations could be more comprehensive in that notice by a placing authority to the area or the approving authority is not required (although notice of approval will have been given). On any subsequent placement therefore, neither the approving nor the area authority will necessarily know of the circumstances although their consent will be required. There may be circumstances short of a reason for termination of approval of the foster parent which justified the placing authority in terminating the placement. That information would not necessarily be available on review and might affect, for example, the age range for which approval was given. The omission of a requirement to notify the approving authority of all terminations is puzzling in view of the fact that they are required to keep a case record including dates on which each placement began and terminated and the circumstances of the termination. That puts a heavy onus on the approving authority to 'chase up' each placement. There should clearly be a duty on all placing authorities to notify termination to the approving authority (if different) and although not prescribed such a procedure should be adopted.

23.21 Parents may remove a child accommodated under *s 20(1)* without notice and foster parents will need to know how any necessary action for the protection of the child may be taken.

23.22 **Short-term placements**

Where a child has a series of placements with the same foster parent within one year, each of no more than four weeks in duration and an aggregate not exceeding ninety days, they are treated as a single placement and visits under the regulations are to be made in the first of the series of placements and again after six months from the date of the first placement commencing.

23.23 **Placements outside England and Wales**

Local authorities may arrange to place outside England and Wales with the approval of every person having parental responsibility [*CA 1989, Sch 2 para 19(2)*]. If the child is in care the leave of the court is required. Voluntary organisations cannot do this. Where the authority makes such arrangements they must ensure so far as is reasonably practicable that the requirements of the regulations are met.

23.24 Foster Parents

23.24 **Emergency and immediate placements** [*reg 11*]

Voluntary organisations have no powers under *reg 11*. In an emergency a local authority may place with any approved foster parent for a period not exceeding 24 hours. The authority must be satisfied it is the most suitable way of performing their duties and obtain a written agreement covering the matters set out in *reg 11(4)* (care as though a member of family, allow visits etc.).

23.25 An immediate placement is one with a person who has not been approved. It is only designed to cover placement with a relative or friend (where the child can be in familiar surroundings) and the authority must obtain a written agreement as in 23.17 FOSTER PLACEMENT AGREEMENT – *reg 5(6)* above and the placement may last for up to six weeks. Before placement the accommodation must be inspected and information obtained about members of the household. Guidance urges authorities to be cautious in the case of this power and that authorisation at a senior level should be required.

23.26 **Arrangement for voluntary organisations to place on behalf of local authority** [*reg 8*]

Arrangements may be made for a voluntary organisation to place on behalf of the local authority. A written agreement must be made about the arrangements for consultation and for exchange of information etc. The authority must be satisfied as to the capacity of the organisation and that the arrangement is the most suitable way of discharging its duties.

23.27 **RECORDS –** *REGULATIONS 12 AND 13*

Authorities must compile a register of each approved foster parent in their area and each relative or friend with whom an immediate placement has been made. The foster parent record will include persons they have been notified are approved by other authorities under *reg 3(3)(b)*.

23.28 Authorities must also compile a case record for foster parents they have approved and relatives or friends with whom a child is given an immediate placement. The case records will include the documentation and a record of each child placed and reasons for termination of placement. A record will also be kept of refusals of approval.

23.29 These records must be kept for at least ten years from the date on which approval is terminated or until death if earlier. In the case of a relative or friend it is suggested that the records are kept for ten years from the date of last placement.

23.30 **LOCAL AUTHORITY VISITS TO CHILDREN PLACED BY VOLUNTARY ORGANISATIONS –** *REGULATIONS 15 AND 16*

A local authority must satisfy itself that any voluntary organisation accommodating a child is satisfactorily safeguarding and promoting the welfare of any children placed in their area or outside that area on their behalf. Children accommodated in a local authority area by or on behalf of a voluntary organisation must be visited from time to time. The minimum requirements are set out in the regulations. Visits are to be made:

(*a*)   within twenty-eight days of placement;

(*b*) on request from the organisation or foster parent, within fourteen days;

(*c*) within seven days if informed the child's welfare may be at risk; or

(*d*) at six-monthly intervals if satisfied as to the welfare of the child.

23.31 As with supervision of placements generally the child should be seen.

23.32 Social workers authorised by the local authority have powers of entry and inspection of premises and records.

23.33 If the authority is not satisfied about the child's welfare they must, if reasonably practicable, take steps to ensure that care is undertaken by a parent, relative or non-parent with parental responsibility.

23.34 THE USUAL FOSTERING LIMIT

The Act prescribes a limit of three children who may be placed at any one time in a foster home. The limit does not apply if the children are all siblings with respect to each other. If the limit is exceeded the foster home is a children's home and must be registered as such unless the authority use their powers to grant exemption [*s 63, Sch 7, paras 2 and 3*].

23.35 The usual limit applies both to local authority and private foster parents.

23.36 Exemption

The authority must consider the number and circumstances of the children, the arrangements for care, the relationship between foster parent and child and the period of time involved, and the welfare of all the children in the household.

23.37 If exemption is granted, notice in writing of the children that may be fostered and any conditions imposed is required. The exemption may be varied or cancelled at any time. Emergency placements are not treated as part of the usual limit. Court exemption is not therefore required for them.

23.38 If the usual limit is exceeded or where exemption is made but a child not named is fostered (unless all are siblings) and the authorised limit is exceeded, the foster parent is treated as carrying on a children's home.

23.39 In considering exemptions the guidance suggests 'pointers' which may indicate that a home is not 'the extension of the family circle which is the hallmark of foster care':

— a fixed number of places are offered;

— all places must be filled to achieve viability;

— investments have been made in the fabric of the building to accommodate a larger number of children;

— a voluntary organisation has arranged for a couple to run an establishment with a view to providing care for a fixed number of children.

24 Guardians

24.1 References
Children Act 1989, ss 5 and 6

24.2 EFFECT OF BEING APPOINTED A GUARDIAN
A guardian of a child has parental responsibility for that child [*s 5(6)*]. However, unlike a parent, a guardian is not considered to be a 'liable relative' for the purposes of the *Social Security Act 1986*, nor may a guardian be made subject to the same orders for property adjustment or financial provision as a parent might be. A guardian has the right to consent or withhold consent to an application to free a child for adoption or to agree or withhold agreement to a child's adoption. Guardians can appoint other guardians to take their place in the event of the guardian's death.

24.3 APPOINTMENT OF GUARDIANS
Guardians can be appointed either privately or by a court order.

24.4 Private appointments
Appointments of guardians can be made by any parent with parental responsibility and any guardian [*s 5(3)(4)*]. A parent or guardian can appoint more than one person to be the child's guardian and the appointment of additional guardians can be made on different occasions. Appointments must be made in writing and signed by the person who makes the appointment [*s 5(5)*]. They are often made by deed or will but do not need to be.

The appointment of a guardian will *only* take effect on the death of the person appointing a guardian if following that death

(*a*) the child has no parent with parental responsibility; or

(*b*) where there is a residence order or custody order under the old law in favour of the person who made the appointment immediately before her/his death unless a residence or existing custody order was also made in favour of the surviving parent.

24.5 Appointment by the court
The High Court, county court or magistrates' court may appoint an individual to be a child's guardian if:

— the child has no parent with parental responsibility for her/him; or

— a residence order has been made in respect of the child in favour of a parent or guardian of her/his who has died while the order was in force [*s 5(1)*];

— the guardian must be an individual and cannot be a body such as the local authority. The court can however appoint more than one guardian.

The application must be made by an individual who wishes to be the guardian although the court could make an appointment of its own motion in existing family proceedings. When making an appointment the court must regard the child's welfare as the paramount consideration and be satisfied that making an order is better than making no order at all.

25 Guardians ad litem

25.1 References

Children Act 1989, ss 41, 42
Guardian ad Litem and Reporting Officers (Panels) Regulations 1991 (SI 1991 No 2051)
Department of Health Manual of Practice guidance for GALROs
Manual of Practice Guidance for GALRO Panel Managers

25.2 APPOINTMENT

The court hearing 'specified proceedings' must itself appoint a guardian for the child 'unless satisfied that it is not necessary to do so in order to safeguard his interests'.

The local authority has a duty to establish a panel of guardians and reporting officers. The authority decides what qualifications and experience will be required and the court must appoint from that panel (or another authority's panel). In establishing a panel the authority must have regard not only to the number of children who may be involved in proceedings but the different racial groups to which they may belong [*reg 4(6), SI 1991 No 2051*].

The guardian selected by the court must not be a member, officer or servant of the local authority (or NSPCC) which is a party to the proceedings or have been as such concerned in arrangements for the child's care in the previous five years or be a serving probation officer. There are exceptions to this rule in that local authorities may now employ a guardian solely as such [*Family Proceedings Courts (Children Act 1989) Rules 1991 (SI 1991 No 1395), r 10(7)(a)*]. This is a radical departure from previous legislation. Further, a part-time probation officer not previously concerned with the child or her/his family may also be selected.

The rules speak of selection from the panel by the court or justices clerk but no doubt arrangements whereby the panel administrator in fact offers a name or names will continue where convenience dictates.

Parties to the proceedings may apply for the appointment of a guardian at any stage without notice, and one must then be appointed by the court unless it is not considered necessary for the child's interests. If the application is refused the court must give its reasons. The court may also at any stage decide to appoint a guardian.

The appointment continues for the time specified or until terminated by the court for reasons given in writing.

25.3 Specified proceedings

The Act and court rules set out the specified proceedings. They include not only care and related proceedings but also applications under *Part V* (Protection of Children) e.g. emergency protection, child assessment, and secure accommodation orders [*CA 89, s 41(6); SI 1991 No 1395, r 2.2* and the *Family Proceedings Rules 1991 (SI 1991 No 1247), r 4.2*].

25.4 POWERS AND DUTIES OF THE GUARDIAN

The guardian's duty is to safeguard the interests of the child in the manner prescribed by the rules of court [*CA 89 s 41(2)* and *SI 1991 No 1395, r 11* and *SI 1991 No 1247, r 4.11*].

Specific duties

(a) To have regard to the general principle that delay is likely to prejudice the welfare of the child and to the particular aspects of a child's welfare (to which the court must have regard) set out in *CA 89, s 1(3)(a)-(f)*.

(b) To appoint a solicitor (unless one has already been appointed), give appropriate advice to the child and instruct the solicitor. Where the child is able to give instructions on her/his own behalf, having regard to her/his understanding and wishes to give instructions which conflict with those of the guardian, the solicitor must take the child's instructions.

(c) To inform the court where the child is instructing the solicitor directly or intends to or is capable of conducting the proceedings on her/his own behalf.

Thereafter all the guardian's duties other than instructing the solicitor remain, unless the court directs otherwise, and the guardian may with leave of the court be her/himself legally represented (but not under legal aid).

(d) To attend, unless excused, all direction appointments in and hearings of the proceedings and give advice on prescribed matters such as the timing, forum, the child's wishes and understanding and options open to the court. Advice may be given, subject to any direction of the court, orally or in writing.

(e) To consider whether any person should be joined as a party and notify such persons of their right, or the clerk of the court of any notification given or attempted, and anyone who the guardian believes may wish to be joined.

(f) To make any necessary investigations and in particular, interview relevant persons or those the court directs, inspect records made by the authority or NSPCC in connection with the application and any other of the child care records. The guardian must notify the court and other persons the court directs of all the records inspected which s/he thinks assist in the proper determination of the court. The guardian has a right at all reasonable times to inspect and take copies of certain records. Her/his duty is to draw the court's attention to those inspected which may give assistance.

(g) To file a written report not less than seven days before the final hearing advising on the child's interests, copies of which the court will serve on the parties.

The law is now much more explicit and also more extensive as regards access to records. The records or parts of them may be at the court's direction brought to the notice of the parties to the proceedings. Further a copy of any record examined is admissible as evidence of any motion referred to in the guardian's written report or oral evidence to the court. It would seem that the principle by which child care records were regarded as privileged from disclosure has been further eroded. Any party may question the guardian on oral or written evidence tendered and this itself may bring about disclosure. GALs are also entitled to access to a

25.5 Guardians ad litem

voluntary organisation's foster parent registers or records (*Foster Placement (Children) Regulations 1991 (SI 1991 No 910), r 14(4)* and children's home records and registers – *Children's Homes Regulations (SI 1991 No 1506), r 16*).

(*h*) To obtain such appropriate professional assistance as is available to her/him or as directed.

(*j*) To provide any other assistance required by the court.

Any statement in the guardian's report and any evidence given as regards matters referred to in the report are admissible irrespective of the hearsay rule to the extent that the court considers it relevant. The report, it would appear, may be considered at any stage in the proceedings. The rules provide a 'normal' order of speeches and evidence subject to any directions given by the court. The normal order set out makes no reference to the guardian's written report, although the court is required to read before the hearing any documentary evidence filed by the parties.

25.5 INDEPENDENCE OF THE GAL

In *R v Cornwall CC ex parte G, The Guardian,* 15 November 1991, the President of the Family Division ruled that it was vitally important that the GALs' position 'should not be compromised by any restriction placed directly or indirectly upon each of them in the carrying out of their duties'. Accordingly restrictions on the number of hours GALs were entitled to spend on each case were quashed.

25.6 LOCAL AUTHORITY PANELS

Each authority must establish a panel but the opportunity remains for groups of authorities to operate together or for contracting out of the running of the panel e.g. a voluntary organisation.

The numbers appointed to the panel must so far as possible be sufficient to service the demands of the courts. A panel administrator must be appointed who is not otherwise involved with the authority's children's services.

25.7 A complaints board and a panel committee must be established to perform the functions assigned by the regulations. The composition of the panels is set out in *Schs 1* and *2 of SI 1991 No 2051*. Complaints about the operation of the panel are first considered by the authority and if not resolved with the complainant, are to be referred to the board for it to make a recommendation. The complaint is notified to the person in respect of whom it is made who will have the opportunity to make representations both to the authority and the board. Having taken into account any recommendation made the authority must give the complainant and 'respondent' written notice of their decision.

The panel committee is the focal point of liaison with the courts and also advises on the standards and practices of GALROs in relevant proceedings, the appointment or reappointment and review of GALROs, the training of GALROs, the matters arising from complaints concerning GALROs (but not investigation of particular complaints).

25.8 The DOH guidance is unhelpful in the contentious area of the panel committee's advice on standards of practice. This is, together with the provision made for training, quite crucial. Attempts to review standards of practice of GALROs will involve issues of confidentiality and may be seen to represent interference with the GALROs independence by the local authority. The problem nevertheless must be faced as the authority itself and not the panel committee has the duty [*reg 10* of *SI 1991 No 2051*] to seek the views of the committee on the work of each panel member and review the work of each member of the panel. Panel records required to be kept by *reg 7* of *SI 1991 No 2051* may give some assistance in this respect but the use of some independent committee members or outsiders may be appropriate.

25.9 Termination of GALROs appointment

The authority may terminate at any time where they consider a GALRO is unable or unfit to carry out a GALRO's functions. An authority must give written reasons to the GALRO for proposing termination and give an opportunity for representations to be made. The matter must then be referred to the complaints board for a recommendation if termination is still pursued.

26 Independent Visitor

26.1 References

Children Act 1989, Sch 2, para 17
Definition of Independent Visitors (Children) Regulations 1991 (SI 1991 No 892)
Department of Health guidance Vol 3 Ch 7 (Vol 4 Ch 6)

26.2 INTRODUCTION

Section 11 of the *Child Care Act 1980* (like its predecessor *CYPA 1969, s 24(5)* has been repealed and replaced by the provisions of the above Schedule and regulations. These are more wide-reaching in that there is no age limit and the scheme applies to children accommodated as well as in care, whether in residential accommodation or otherwise. Further, a child of sufficient understanding may refuse a proposed appointment or bring one to an end.

26.3 DUTY TO APPOINT

Every child looked after by a local authority must have an independent visitor appointed where:

(a) communication between the child and parent or non-parent with parental responsibility has been 'infrequent'; or

(b) the child has not been visited by (or lived with) any such person during the preceding twelve months; and

(c) the local authority believe it would be in the child's best interests.

The regulations define who is not independent of the local authority. This includes local authority members, officers, and members' employees of an organisation providing accommodation and their spouses. The DOH advises the take up of references and checks with the police for previous convictions including 'exempt' convictions under the *Rehabilitation of Offenders Act 1974* and reference to the DOH Consultancy Service.

The duty to appoint may arise wherever the child (of any age) is accommodated. If the child is fostered and has contact with family members, though not parents, the child's 'best interests' might not necessarily be served by an independent visitor.

26.4 Consultation

At reviews, authorities must consider whether it is appropriate to appoint a visitor and take into account the child's views and those of her/his parents etc. It would be advisable to involve a visitor in the reviews. The child's views on appointment and termination must also be sought as a child of 'sufficient understanding' has the right to object to a proposed appointment or its continuation. If the child objects, the appointment cannot be made, or if made, must be determined.

26.5 DUTIES

The visitor's duty is to visit, advise and befriend the child. Reasonable expenses incurred for those purposes may be recovered from the authority. Authorities may find it helpful to offer guidelines to visitors on the way in which claims for expenses will be handled.

26.6 TERMINATION

Apart from the child's objection the appointment of a visitor is determined if the visitor or authority gives notice to that effect in writing. The authority is not required to state its reasons. The visitor may be able to make use of the complaints and representations procedure under *s 26(3)* of the *CA 89* if the authority consider a visitor as having 'sufficient interest in the child's welfare to warrant his representations being considered by them' or any other complaint procedure established by the authority.

27 Legal Aid

27.1 References

Children Act 1989, s 99
Legal Aid Act 1988, ss 15, 19, 22 and *Sch 2, para 2*
The Legal Aid Act 1988 (Children Act 1989) Order 1991 (SI 1991 No 1924)
Legal Aid in Criminal and Care Proceedings (General) (Amendment) No 2 Regulations 1991 (SI 1991 No 1925)

27.2 CIVIL PROCEEDINGS

Legal aid in any proceedings under the *Children Act 1989* now forms part of civil legal aid. As regards care and related proceedings the position is summarised in the Table of provisions below.

Summary Table of provisions/civil legal aid in care proceedings

Proceedings	Parties	Means/merits waived	Section
ss 31, 43, 44 and *45*	child, parents, parental responsibility	means and merits	15(3C)
appeal of care proceedings	as above	means	15(3D)
application to join/joined as party to *ss 31, 43, 44* and *45*	any	merits	15(3E)

Civil legal aid is normally granted subject to the merits of the application and to the means of the applicant. Local authorities cannot be granted legal aid for the purposes of any proceedings under the *Children Act 1989*. Certain other bodies may be excluded by regulations if and when made.

Proceedings for care or supervision orders, child assessment, emergency protection orders, or extension or discharge of an emergency protection order now fall within the provisions for civil legal aid. The Table above shows that certain applications must be granted irrespective of capital and income limits (means test) set out in the relevant regulations. Other applications must be granted irrespective of whether it is thought there are reasonable grounds for being a party to the proceedings (merits) – for example, joinder, but are subject to the means test. On appeal against an order made in care proceedings legal aid must be granted irrespective of means provided there are reasonable grounds for the appeal.

Regardless of means or merits where an application for a secure accommodation order is made, a child who is not, but wishes to be, legally represented must be granted legal aid.

In all other proceedings civil legal aid is available subject to means and merits.

27.3 CRIMINAL PROCEEDINGS

Applications to vary/discharge a supervision order made in criminal proceedings under *ss 15* and *16(8)* of *CYPA 1969* fall within the scope of criminal legal aid

Legal Aid 27.3

and are subject to both a merits test (desirable in the interests of justice) and a contribution order. *Section 22* of the *Legal Aid Act 1988* sets out the criteria for judging merits (e.g. loss of liberty, livelihood, etc.).

Supervision orders under the 1969 Act will now only be made in criminal proceedings for an offence (a court can no longer make care orders for an offence or on discharge of a supervision order made under *s 7(7)* of *CYPA 1969* for an offence). *Section 15* of *CYPA 1969* does not apply to supervision orders made under *s 31* of the *Children Act 1989* to which *Parts I* and *II* of *Sch 3* to the 1989 Act apply. Applications to vary a *s 31* order are within the scope of civil legal aid, and subject to the means and merits tests.

28 Parental Responsibility

28.1 References
Children Act 1989, ss 2, 3 and *4*

28.2 DEFINITION

Parental responsibility is defined in *s 3(1)* of the Act as meaning 'all the rights, duties, powers, responsibilities and authority which by law a parent of a child has in relation to the child and his property'. It replaces the concept of 'parental rights', which in any event had never been defined in any detail, and which, over the years, had come to have little significance. The courts had stated that in reality parental rights were little more than a collection of powers and duties which existed as a result of being a parent with responsibility for bringing up a child. English law never defined those powers and duties except in very specific ways, for example by providing that a parent had the right to consent to a child's adoption. Much was and is left to a parent's discretion except that it is an offence to neglect or ill-treat a child and the civil law has for a long time enabled the courts to intervene to protect children.

The *Children Act 1989* does not define parental responsibility in any more specific way than previous legislation and case law, but does provide a consistent framework for deciding who acquires it, how it can be exercised and what effect an order under the Act will have on it.

28.3 EFFECT OF PARENTAL RESPONSIBILITY

Parental responsibility enables the person or persons with it to take most of the decisions relating to the child's life, for example, where the child is to live, go to school and so on. This is tempered by other legislation, for example by the Education Acts which limit parental freedom to educate a child. It is also limited by some of the provisions in the *Children Act 1989* itself.

28.4 Day to day care

A person with parental responsibility for a child will be able to make most of the day to day decisions relating to the child's care. These include decisions regarding clothing, diet, activities, where to go for holidays, pocket money, Saturday and holiday jobs etc. All of this is, however, subject to the requirements of the law that it is a criminal offence to ill-treat or neglect a child (see the requirements of the Education Acts and the legislation governing the employment of children).

A person with parental responsibility can arrange for some or all of that responsibility to be met by others [*s 2(9)*]. This would cover arranging for a childminder to look after a child (see also REGISTRATION AND INSPECTION (33)), babysitters etc. Private fostering arrangements are also lawful by virtue of this section, although they are subject to specific regulation under the Act (see PRIVATE FOSTERING (31)).

If more than one person has parental responsibility for a child they will need to try and agree the arrangements made for the child. For example, where married

Parental Responsibility 28.10

parents are living together such decisions are made on a continuous basis. Disputes do arise, most commonly where parents have separated. If the disagreement cannot be resolved by the adults concerned they can ask the court to intervene by making one of the *s 8* orders (see SECTION 8 ORDERS (41)).

28.5 Education

The law lays down minimum standards for the education of children which those with parental responsibility must comply with.

28.6 Appointment of a guardian

See GUARDIANS (24).

28.7 Religious upbringing

The law imposes no duty to give a child a religious upbringing and the person with parental responsibility has the right to determine the child's upbringing although it is clear that this will cease when the child is of an age to form her/his own views.

28.8 Medical treatment

In general terms, anyone, including the local authority, who has parental responsibility for a child can give a valid consent for any medical treatment. In emergencies a doctor can undertake treatment if the child's well-being could suffer because of the delay that would be caused in obtaining consent for treatment. A child who is over 16 may consent to any surgical, medical or dental treatment [*Family Law Reform Act 1969, s 8(1)*]. This provision however does not mean that children under the age of 16 cannot give valid consent to medical treatment. The case of *Gillick v West Norfolk and Wisbeach Area Health Authority and the Department of Health and Social Security (1986) AC 112* established that a child of sufficient age and understanding, even if under 16, could give valid consent. The position is complex, however, and it is likely to be the subject of further litigation. If an issue arises regarding medical treatment, it would be sensible to take legal advice.

28.9 Adoption

Only a parent with parental responsibility or a guardian has the right to agree or refuse to agree a child's adoption. It follows that the mother of a child will always have the right to agree or refuse to agree, as will the married father of a child. The unmarried father of a child will also acquire the right if he has a parental responsibility order or agreement. The child's guardian also has the right to do so.

28.10 Passports

Normally the passport authorities will require the consent of either a married parent or the unmarried mother of a child before issuing a passport to a child. It is possible to obtain an order objecting to the issue of a passport to a child. Such an order could be a specific issue order or a prohibitive steps order. If such an order is granted then it is open to anyone with parental responsibility to ask the passport agency not to issue a passport. Further details can be obtained from the United Kingdom Passport Agency, Clive House, Petty France, London SW1H 9HD.

28.11 Parental Responsibility

28.11 **Consent to marry**

A child under 16 cannot contract a valid marriage. Those between 16 and 18 can but will need the consent of the appropriate adult. These are as follows:

— Children who are not subject to any existing orders will need the consent of each parent who has parental responsibility and each guardian where:

(i) there is or was in force immediately before the child's 16th birthday a residence order; the required consent is that of the person with whom the child lived, or was living, or supposed to live as a result of the order; or

(ii) the child is subject to a care order, the required consent is that of the local authority, each parent with parental responsibility and each guardian.

28.12 One feature of the new law is that parental responsibility can be shared. Married parents always share it, but others can also acquire it in which case they share it with the parent or parents of a child. The mother of an illegitimate child or the parents of a legitimate child only lose parental responsibility when an adoption order is made. Those who can acquire parental responsibility are listed in 28.14 ACQUISITION OF PARENTAL RESPONSIBILITY below.

Others who acquire parental responsibility can lose it. For example a local authority acquires parental responsibility for a child when a care order is made but loses it if the care order is discharged. A non-parent looking after a child under a residence order acquires parental responsibility whilst the order is in force but loses it when the order ceases to have effect. Parental responsibility cannot be passed on or given up to someone else. However, the Act provides that the exercise of parental responsibility can be delegated [s 2(9)]. This would apply, for example, where a parent was going into hospital and arranged for someone else to look after the child during that time. A person who has the care of the child but who does not have parental responsibility may do whatever is reasonable for safeguarding or promoting the child's welfare [s 3(5)]. Where more than one person has parental responsibility for a child, that responsibility can be met by one of those concerned acting independently of the others [s 2(5) and (7)]. Where disputes occur in the exercise of that responsibility they can be resolved by applying to the court for a specific issue or prohibited steps order. The position is different where a child is in the care of a local authority since the local authority has the power to determine the extent to which a parent can meet her/his parental responsibility (see 28.14 ACQUISITION OF PARENTAL RESPONSIBILITY below).

28.13 **MARRIED PARENTS**

Married parents each have parental responsibility [s 2(1)]. If parents marry after their child is born the father acquires parental responsibility as if the parents had been married at the time of their child's birth [s 2(3)]. An unmarried mother has sole parental responsibility for her child although the father can acquire it.

28.14 **ACQUISITION OF PARENTAL RESPONSIBILITY**

The father of an illegitimate child

The father of an illegitimate child can acquire parental responsibility in four ways.

Parental Responsibility 28.14

(a) By marrying the child's mother. This happens automatically on the father's marriage to the mother and so no application to the court is needed.

(b) By entering into a parental responsibility agreement [*s 4*]. A parental responsibility agreement is intended to be a simple way of acquiring parental responsibility without the need for court proceedings. It must be made on a specified form and in accordance with the procedures laid down by parliament (see the *Parental Responsibility Agreement Regulations 1991 (SI 1991 No 1478)*. It is likely to be used by couples living in a stable relationship who for whatever reason do not wish to get married.

(c) By applying to the court for a parental responsibility order [*s 4*]. This is likely to be used where there is no agreement between the parents. In addition, a father in whose favour a residence order is made (see SECTION 8 ORDERS (41)) will always acquire parental responsibility for the child. If the residence order is later discharged the father will not lose parental responsibility unless the court specifically orders this.

(d) By being appointed the child's guardian (see GUARDIANS (24)).

A person in whose favour a residence order has been made

The court can make residence orders in favour of those who are not parents (see SECURE ACCOMMODATION (41)). Where this is done, the person in whose favour the residence order is made acquires parental responsibility, but only whilst the residence order remains in force [*s 12(2)*].

Guardians

Guardians acquire parental responsibility when their appointment takes effect [*s 5(6)*]. (For more about guardians see GUARDIANS (24)).

Local authorities and those who have obtained emergency protection orders

Anyone who obtains an emergency protection order acquires parental responsibility for the child for as long as the order remains in force. This is limited however to taking action reasonably required to safeguard or promote the child's welfare [see *ss 44(4)* and *44(5)*]. Where a child is in the care of a local authority under a care order, the local authority acquires parental responsibility and can decide the extent to which the child's parent or guardian should meet that responsibility [*s 33(3)*]. The powers of local authorities in relation to children in care are dealt with in CARE AND SUPERVISION ORDERS (3) which should be read in conjunction with this. Local authorities do not acquire parental responsibility for children whom they are accommodating.

Adoptive parents

Adoptive parents acquire parental responsibility on the making of an adoption order [see *Sch 10, para 3* which amends *s 12* of the *Adoption Act 1976*].

Adoption Agencies

An Adoption Agency acquires parental responsibility for a child in respect of whom an order has been made freeing her/him for adoption [see *Sch 10, para 6* which amends *s 18* of the *Adoption Act 1976*].

29 Parties to Proceedings

29.1 **References**

Children Act 1989, s 41(6)
Family Proceedings Courts (Children Act 1989) Rules 1991, (SI 1991 No 1395), rr 2(2) and 7 and Sch 2
Family Proceedings Rules 1991, (SI 1991 No 1247), rr 4(2), 4 and 7

29.2 The parties to proceedings under the *Children Act* are set out in the court rules. The rules are complex and prescribe who may make certain applications and govern procedures generally. Both sets of rules allow any person to request that s/he or another person be joined as a party or cease to be a party. Further, a Guardian ad litem may advise joinder of parties. Recognition of the child as a party in certain proceedings is given in the Act which also specifies proceedings in which, under the rules, the child must be a party. These are any proceedings:

(a) for an application for a care or supervision order;

(b) in which the court has given a direction under *s 37(1)* (local authority directed to investigate) and has made or is considering whether to make an interim care order;

(c) on an application for the discharge of a care order or the variation or discharge of a supervision order;

(d) on an application under *s 39(4)* (substitution of supervision order on discharge of care order);

(e) in which the court is considering whether to make a residence order with respect to a child who is the subject of a care order;

(f) with respect to contact between a child who is the subject of a care order and any other person;

(g) under *Part V (Protection of Children)*;

(h) on an appeal against the making or refusal to make an order under (a) or (d) above or any order under *s 34*, and the variation, discharge or refusal to vary or discharge any such orders; the refusal of an application under *s 39(4)*; or the making or refusal of an order under *Part V*; or

(j) which are specified by rules of court.

These so far are:

— proceedings under *s 25* (secure accommodation);

— applications under *s 33(7)* (new surname, removal from UK of child in care);

— proceedings under *para 19(1)* of *CA 89 Sch 2* (approval of children in care to live outside England and Wales);

— applications under *para 6(3)* of *CA 89 Sch 3* (supervisors' application to extend supervision order);

— proceedings for an education supervision order;

— application to extend education supervision order; and

Parties to Proceedings 29.4

— discharge of education supervision order.

Reference should be made to the rules as respects parties other than children. This section does not set out to deal with detailed procedural provisions, but singles out children because of the importance attached to recognition of their rights and the concern expressed during debate on the legislation for a more consistent approach to the child as party to the proceedings concerning her/himself.

29.3 ORDERS

It is significant that a child is not as of right a respondent to applications for a *s 8* order (see SECTION 8 ORDERS (41)). Courts are given power to direct that a person who would not otherwise be a respondent, be joined as a party and a guardian *ad litem* may well encourage such action. While any request to be joined as a party by a person with parental responsibility must be granted there is no corresponding provision, for example, for a 'child of sufficient understanding'.

29.4 Child as applicant

A child may apply for a *s 8* order with the leave of the court, but this may only be granted if the court is satisfied s/he has sufficient understanding to make the application [*s 10(8)*]. A child may also apply for an order for contact under *s 34(2)*, discharge of an education supervision order under *Sch 3, para 17(1)*, or discharge of a care or supervision order under *s 39(1)* or *s 39(2)*. There is no specific provision corresponding to *s 70(2)* of the *CYPA 1969* (now repealed except for discharge/variation of pre-1989 Act supervision orders) which allowed a parent or guardian to make applications on behalf of the child although those with parental responsibility for the child may make applications in their own right. Nor has the child yet been prescribed by rules made under *s 10(7)* as entitled to apply for any *s 8* order (the rules may prescribe any category of persons as entitled to apply for any prescribed *s 8* order).

30 Privacy

30.1 **References**

Children Act 1989, s 97
Children and Young Persons Act 1933, s 39
Family Proceedings Rules 1991 (SI 1991 No 1247)
Family Proceedings Courts (Children Act 1989) Rules 1991 (SI 1991 No 1395)

30.2 Publication of any material intended or likely to identify a child in any proceedings before a magistrates' court in which any power under the 1989 Act may be used with respect to any child is an offence. It is a defence to show that the accused did not know and had no reason to suspect that publication would lead to the child's identification [s 97].

30.3 The restrictions on reporting apply also to radio, television and cable broadcasting [s 97(5) of the 1989 Act as amended by the *Broadcasting Act 1990*].

30.4 Legislation regarding the prohibition of reporting in proceedings before other courts is unchanged [see s 39 of CYPA 1933].

30.5 The court can make an order that proceedings should take place in the absence of any party including the child if it considers it to be in the child's interests, and the party who is not to be present is represented by a solicitor or Guardian ad litem.

30.6 Family proceedings courts can also make an order that proceedings be heard in private if it is considered that would be in the child's interests. In that case only the court's officers, the parties, their legal representatives and anyone else specified by the court can attend [*SI 1991 No 1247 r 4.16* and *SI 1991 No 1395 r 16*].

30.7 Proceedings in the county court or High Court are automatically heard in private (in chambers) unless the court otherwise directs [*SI 1991 No 1247 r 4.16(7)*].

31 Private Fostering

31.1 References

Children Act 1989, Part IX and *Schs 7* and *8*
Children (Private Arrangements for Fostering) Regulations 1991 (SI 1991 No 2050)
Disqualification for Caring for Children Regulations 1991 (SI 1991 No 2094)

31.2 BACKGROUND

Previous legislation in the *Foster Children Act 1980* has been repealed and the detail replaced with modifications in the 1991 regulations. Local authoritiy functions are similar to those in the 1980 Act, but the authority's welfare duties are now broadly the same as for children living in voluntary registered children's homes. Consistency is also achieved by the application of the 'usual fostering limit' (see 23.34 THE USUAL FOSTERING LIMIT) and the ability to use emergency protection orders, for example, in place of the power, now repealed, to remove a child from her/his placement.

A major change is that private placements for less than 28 days even if with a 'regular foster parent' are no longer classed as private fostering. Placement for under 28 days of children under eight years for reward are covered by the childminding provisions of the 1989 Act.

31.3 DEFINITION OF PRIVATELY FOSTERED CHILDREN

A privately fostered child is one who is:

(a) under 16 (or under 18 if disabled). This allows the provisions of *s 24(2)* (After Care) to be applied to disabled children;

(b) cared for and accommodated by a person who is not her/his parent or relative, or person with parental responsibility; or

(c) cared for for at least 28 days (or less if the intention is to stay for that period or longer);

but not one who is:

(d) being looked after by a local authority;

(e) living in premises in which any parent, person with parental responsibility or relative who has assumed responsibility for her/his care is for the time being living;

(f) in accommodation provided by or on behalf of a voluntary organisation;

(g) accommodated in a school providing full-time education, hospital or a registered home;

(h) in the care of a person as a result of the requirement of a supervision order [*s 7(7)(b)* of the *CYPA 1969*];

(j) liable to be detained or subject to guardianship under the *Mental Health Act 1983*;

31.4 Private Fostering

(k) placed by an adoption agency in the care of a person who proposes to adopt her/him;

(l) is a protected child under the *Adoption Act 1976*.

31.4 Notices required

Notice in writing must be given to the local authority by the proposed foster parent, anyone else involved in the arrangements and any parent who knows of the arrangement, even if not involved. Notice must be given no less than 6 weeks or more than 13 weeks before the child is placed. Emergency placements may be made but must be notified within 48 hours.

31.5 Content of the notice

Religious persuasion, racial origin and cultural and linguistic background are included in the specific information required, together with, for example, details of any previous convictions (subject to the *Rehabilitation of Offenders Act 1974*).

31.6 LOCAL AUTHORITY POWERS AND DUTIES – *Children Act 1989, s 67; Children (Private Arrangements for Fostering) Regulations 1991 (SI 1991 No 2050), reg 2*

Welfare

Authorities must satisfy themselves that the child's welfare is being satisfactorily safeguarded and promoted and ensure that any necessary advice is given to the carer. The specifics of welfare are set out in *reg 2* and include *inter alia* inquiry as to whether the child's religious, racial etc. needs are being met, as well as ascertaining the child's wishes and feelings.

The child must be visited at such intervals as considered necessary and when reasonably requested by the child or foster parent, but in the first year, within one week of the placement and then at least every six weeks. In subsequent years the child must be visited at least every three months. A written report on each visit should be made to the authority. Arrangements should also be made to see the child alone. Where there is reasonable cause to believe a privately fostered child is being accommodated, or it is proposed to accommodate such a child, any person authorised to visit private foster children may inspect the premises and children at any reasonable time.

The premises and any child present may be inspected at any reasonable time by any person authorised by the local authority.

31.7 Prohibition of private fostering

The local authority may prohibit the foster parent or proposed foster parent from fostering any child, any particular child or in any particular premises if of the opinion that the foster parent:

(a) is not suitable;

(b) the premises are not suitable; or

(c) the placement or contemplated placement would be prejudicial to the child's welfare.

Prohibitions may be imposed (e.g. as to premises [*CA 89 s 69*] at the same time as requirements are imposed under *Sch 8* (see below). Written notice must be given by the authority with reasons and information about the right of appeal under *Sch 8*. Prohibitions may be revoked by the authority of their own motion or on application.

31.8 Power to impose requirements

Requirements may be made or varied or revoked regarding numbers, age, sex and arrangements for care and standards of accommodation and equipment. Notice of requirements must be given in writing explaining the right of appeal under *Sch 8* (see 31.10 below) [*Sch 8 para 6*].

31.9 Action to safeguard welfare

Where the authority is not satisfied that a child's welfare is being satisfactorily safeguarded or promoted there is no specific power to remove the child by application to a court as under the repealed *Foster Children Act 1980*. The provisions for protection of children (care order, supervision order etc.) are available. The authority have a duty to take reasonably practicable steps to see that a parent, person with parental responsibility or relative undertakes the child's care and consider whether any other powers under the 1989 Act should be exercised (e.g. application for care order, provision of support services etc.).

31.10 Appeals against prohibitions/requirements

Appeals against requirements and prohibitions etc. may be made to the magistrates' court which has certain powers to vary or modify any requirement or prohibition made [*Sch 8 para 8*].

31.11 Children living in schools during school holidays

A non-maintained school (which is not by virtue of *s 63(5)(6)* a children's home) may be subject to a requirement to give notice of private fostering if children live in the school for more than two weeks during school holidays. The authority may exempt the school from giving notice and has no power to impose requirements. The schedule is quite burdensome as notice must be given where the child dies or for any other reason ceases to be treated as a privately fostered child. The authority has a duty to visit within one week and make a written report [*SI 1991 No 2050, reg 3*] and this is so seemingly even if exemption from notice is given [*CA Sch 8 para 9*].

31.12 Termination of placement

The foster parent must give notice within 48 hours unless the arrangement is to continue after a break of no more than 27 days. The notice must tell the authority the name and address of the new 'carer'. Death of the child requires immediate notification. Parents and those with parental responsibility must also give notice though no time limit is set.

31.13 Advertisements

Prospective foster parents advertising their services must state their name and address. Publishers as well as the foster parents are liable for any infringement of this provision [*SI 1991 No 2050, reg 10*].

31.14 Private Fostering

31.14 Offences

The section creates a number of summary offences which include refusal to allow visits and failure to comply with requirements or breach of prohibitions [*s 70*].

32 Race, Religion, Culture and Linguistic Background

32.1 **References**

United Nations Convention on the Rights of the Child 1989 (HMSO Cm 1668), Article 20(3)
Children Act 1989, ss 1, 22(5)(c), 33(6), 53(2)(b), 61(3)(c), 64(3)(c), 74(1)(b),(2)(b) and (6), Sch 2, paras 11 and 12(e)
Arrangements for Placement of Children (General) Regulations 1991 (SI 1991 No 890), Sch 4, para 5(a)
Placement of Children with Parents etc. Regulations 1991 (SI 1991 No 893), Sch 1, para 1(h)
Children's Homes Regulations 1991 (SI 1991 No 1506), reg 11, Sch 1, para 9, Sch 2, paras 3 and 4
Children (Private Arrangements for Fostering) Regulations 1991 (SI 1991 No 2050), regs 2(2)(c) and 4(3)
Guardian Ad Litem and Reporting Officers (Panels) Regulations 1991 (SI 1991 No 2051), reg 4(6)
Foster Placement (Children) Regulations 1991 (SI 1991 No 910), reg 5(2)(a) and (b), Sch 1, para 5 and Sch 3, para 1(b)

32.2 **INTRODUCTION**

The importance of a child's religious upbringing has been recognised in a variety of statutory provisions for some time. Approved School Rules, Adoption Acts, *Children Act 1948* and the *Children and Young Persons Act 1969* all made reference to maintaining religious persuasion. The references above demonstrate that far more attention is now paid to all the needs a child may have. The Act and regulations address 'race, religion, culture and linguistic background' (consistent with the wording of the UN Convention) in ascertaining the wishes and needs of the child. The aim is to ensure continuity in as many aspects of the child's life as possible. 'Same race' placement therefore should always be considered as one of the issues in assessment, the significance of which will vary according to the individual needs of the child, and, to an extent, her/his parents. The list is not intended to be exhaustive of the duties of local authorities, foster parents and other carers to have regard to these needs. When considering a child's 'family background', 'welfare', 'particular needs', or 'suitability' of a home or foster parent, race, religion etc. will be equally significant. The specific provisions cited call attention to the duty to identify and record these characteristics, take account of them in making decisions, and act on them in providing care.

32.3 The recruitment of foster parents from different racial groups is made a local authority duty [*Sch 2 para 11*]; day care provision must also take account of the racial groups to which children belong, and registration may be cancelled if the day care is inadequate for the needs of the child having regard to her/his race, religion etc. [*Sch 2 para 11*]. However there is no corresponding provision for the recruitment of residential staff. Nor does the Department of Health guidance (Vol 4) deal with this aspect of staffing. In contrast the regulations require local authorities to have regard to the different racial groups in their areas when appointing GALs and Reporting Officers (see GUARDIANS AD LITEM (25)).

32.4 Race, Religion, Culture and Linguistic Background

32.4 MAKING DECISIONS

Local authorities, voluntary homes and children's homes must give due consideration to race, religion etc. when making the following decisions affecting a child:

— any decision relating to a child being looked after by a local authority [*s 22(5)*]

— any decision relating to a child accommodated by or on behalf of a voluntary organisation [*s 61(3)*].

Where a court is being asked to make, vary or discharge any order under *Part IV* of the Act or an order under *section 8* where the application is opposed it must take into account the child's age, sex, background and any characteristics the court considers relevant [*s 1(3)* 'welfare checklist']. It is generally thought that the child's race, religion, culture and linguistic background are relevant characteristics.

32.5 PROVIDING ADEQUATE CARE

The other provisions cited deal with the way in which the child's needs are to be met, recruitment of foster parents, arrangements for religious observance etc. and the monitoring of those arrangements.

32.6 UNITED NATIONS CONVENTION ON THE RIGHTS OF THE CHILD

Under *Article 20(3)* of the Convention (which has now been adopted by the UK), when a child is temporarily or permanently 'deprived of his or her family environment' and alternative care is required, states shall pay 'due regard to the desirability of continuity in a child's upbringing and to the child's ethnic, religious, cultural and linguistic background'. While the Government may have reservations about other Articles of the Convention, in the light of the above, the requirements of *Article 20* appear to have been met.

33 Registration and Inspection – Day Care

33.1 References

Children Act 1989, ss 18, 71–79 and *Sch 9*
Department of Health guidance Vol 2
Childminding and Day Care (Applications for Registration) Regulations 1991 (SI 1991 No 1689) (as amended by *SI 1991 No 2129*)
Childminding and Day Care (Registration and Inspection Fees) Regulations 1991 (SI 1991 No 2076) (as amended by *SI 1991 No 2129*)
Disqualification for Caring for Children Regulations 1991 (SI 1991 No 2094)

33.2 DEFINITIONS

A 'childminder' is a person who looks after one or more children under eight years, for reward, for more than two hours in any one day, in domestic premises. Even though individual children may be looked after for less than two hours, the time limit refers collectively to the activity of looking after children. Domestic premises should be construed as premises wholly or mainly used as a private dwelling.

A parent or relative of the child, a person with parental responsibility or a foster parent, is not treated as acting as a childminder for the purposes of the registration provisions of the Act. Foster parent includes a local authority, private foster parent and a foster parent for a child placed by a voluntary organisation.

N.B. A private placement for less than 28 days with a foster parent is treated as childminding and not private fostering [*CA 89 s 66(2)(a)*].

Where a person is employed as a nanny s/he is not acting as a childminder when looking after the child wholly or mainly in the home of the person so employing her/him, and this is so where a nanny is employed by two (but no more) different employers to look after children wholly or mainly in the home of either employer. A nanny is defined as one employed to look after a child by a parent, non-parent with parental responsibility, or relative who has assumed responsibility for the care. The term nanny will cover the use of babysitters as well as the more usual meaning of the word.

'Day care' means any form of day care or supervised activity provided for children during the day (whether or not it is provided on a regular basis). Supervised activity means an activity supervised by a responsible person. Day care would include, therefore, creche, play groups, day nurseries, out of school provision, adventure playgrounds, organised leisure activities and holiday schemes. As with childminders, a person does not provide day care unless the period or total periods during which children are looked after exceeds two hours in any day.

33.3 PERSONS REQUIRING REGISTRATION

Persons requiring registration include childminders and persons providing day care for children under the age of eight other than on domestic premises. Premises include any vehicle, for example, a play bus. There is no longer

33.4 Registration and Inspection – Day Care

provision for registration of premises as distinct from persons and no registration is required for day care provisions for children over eight but below the upper limit of compulsory school age.

33.4 Exemption from the requirement to register

The definition of childminder exempts a number of categories of individuals from the requirement to register. However many of the different forms of day care, even though not provided on a regular basis or for reward, are so subject. *Schedule 9* grants exemptions to certain schools, other establishments and the use of occasional facilities.

Exempt Schools

Local education authority maintained and assisted schools, schools under the management of an education authority, independent grant aided schools, grant maintained and self-governing schools and play centres maintained or assisted by a local education authority are exempt if the provision of day care is made by the person carrying on the establishment as part of the establishment's activities, or by a person employed to work at that establishment and authorised to make that provision as part of the establishment's activities.

Other exempt establishments

Registered children's homes, voluntary homes, community homes, homes registered under the *Registered Homes Act 1984* and health service hospitals are exempt where the day care provision is made by the department or person carrying on the establishment as part of its activities or by a person employed to work and authorised to make that provision as part of the establishment's activities.

Occasional facilities

Where day care is provided on less than six days in any year the facilities are exempt provided notice is given to the local authority in writing before the first occasion on which the premises are so used in that year. Facilities, such as those provided at conferences for example, may therefore be exempt.

33.5 CONSEQUENCES OF NON-REGISTRATION

It is an offence to provide day care for children under eight years old unless registered by the local authority. An unregistered childminder may be served with an enforcement notice requiring the minder to register. The notice has effect for one year from the day on which it is served. Contravention of the notice without reasonable excuse is an offence and this is so even though the subsequent contravention occurs in the area of another local authority. Department of Health guidance advises local authorities to give publicity to the requirement to register and where to go for information.

33.6 THE APPLICATION FOR REGISTRATION

The *Childminding and Day Care (Applications for Registration) Regulations 1991 (SI 1991 No 1689)* prescribe the form of statement which the application must contain with respect to the applicant and any persons assisting or likely to be assisting in looking after children, or living or likely to be living on the premises in question, otherwise the application will be of no effect. Each premises to be used to provide day care must be the subject of a separate application and each application is subject to the prescribed fee [*SI 1991 No 2076*]. The local authority must register the person providing day care or acting as childminder if the application is properly made and they are not otherwise entitled to refuse registration. Department of Health guidance suggests that registration could be completed within three months in the case of a childminder and sessional day care, or six months in the case of full day care provision.

The form of application itself is not prescribed by the regulations, but the information to be supplied is set out in *SI 1991 No 1689* and Department of Health guidance which includes details of criminal convictions of those applying to work with children.

33.7 REFUSAL OF REGISTRATION

Fit persons

The local authority may refuse registration if:

(*a*) the applicant, in the case of childminding, or any person looking after any children on the premises concerned, is not fit to look after children under the age of eight; or

(*b*) any person living or likely to be living on the premises, or any person employed or likely to be employed on the premises is not fit to be in the proximity of children under the age of eight.

The local authority should have regard to the following points when considering whether someone is fit to look after children aged under eight:

— previous experience qualifications/training;

— ability to provide warm and consistent care;

— knowledge of and attitude to multi-cultural issues and people of different racial groups;

— physical health, commitment and knowledge to treat all children as individuals and with equal concern;

— mental stability, integrity and flexibility; and

— known involvement in criminal cases involving abuse of children.

With persons living or working on the premises regard should be had to previous record and 'known involvement in criminal cases involving abuse of children'.

'Known involvement' is an unusual concept. Most child abuse giving rise to care proceedings will amount to an offence even though prosecution cannot be brought for a variety of reasons. Restriction to criminal cases seems illogical if the root of the objection is involvement in abuse. On the other hand, the phrase may be far too encompassing, taking in 'known to the police but never tested in court'. Spouses and partners of those proved to be abusers might also be considered as included in such a phrase. The fairness of administrative decisions can be litigated by judicial review but it would seem far more satisfactory to be satisfied by evidence which the applicant has the opportunity to challenge, of actions or omissions which render a person unsuitable to look after young children irrespective of the criminal process. The Department of Health advise that registration must not be refused without obtaining the views of the legal department is salutary in this respect.

33.8 Registration and Inspection – Day Care

Disqualified persons

Schedule 9, CA 89 and *SI 1991 No 2094* set out the persons who may not be registered.

— Any person who lives in the same household as a person who is her/himself disqualified by the regulations, or in a household in which any such person is employed, is disqualified, unless s/he has disclosed the fact to the local authority and obtained their written consent.

— A person disqualified must not provide day care or be concerned in the management of day care or have any financial interest in any provision of day care unless s/he has disclosed the fact to the local authority and obtained their written consent.

Premises

A local authority may refuse to register an applicant if satisfied that the premises concerned are not fit to be used for looking after children under the age of eight, because of their condition, or the condition of any equipment used on the premises, or for any reason connected with their situation, construction or size. Local authorities are advised to check that planning permission has been granted or is not required. Decisions on registration are of course reached independently of those on planning permission. There is no statutory requirement for a local authority to consult the fire service although they are advised by the Department of Health to do so.

The guidance sets out matters to which the local authority should have regard (which include fire safety) and specifically state that 'an intending childminder who lives in a flat above ground level must not be refused registration on the grounds that the premises are not fit because they are above street level and/or outside play space is not adjacent'. Local authorities are asked to pay attention to the arrangements for a child to play outside and to preventing unsupervised access to stairs and lifts, and to ensuring children are unable to leave the premises unsupervised.

Advice is also given on space standards etc. and factors to be taken into account as regards non-domestic premises. As with childminders, the Department of Health considers there is no objection to having a day care facility above the ground floor and registration should not be refused on those grounds alone – 'the local authority will need to pay particular attention to access to the building and outside play space and the safety of the stairs'.

Equipment

The Department of Health has given advice on the safety of equipment and draws attention *inter alia* to conforming to British standards where they exist and environmental health regulations.

33.8 REGISTRATION REQUIREMENTS

Certain requirements must be imposed on the applicant by the local authority. In addition the local authority 'shall impose such reasonable requirements as they consider appropriate in his case'. Regulations may also make provision for other requirements which must be imposed and those which must not. Any requirement may at any time be varied or removed or additional requirements imposed.

Registration and Inspection – Day Care 33.8

Non-domestic premises – mandatory requirements

(*a*)   The maximum number of children, or the maximum number of children within specified age groups, who may be looked after on the premises. In determining this the local authority must take account of the number of children who may at any time be on the premises. The Department of Health does not lay down an upper limit to the numbers in any type of day care or supervised activity. Factors to be considered include the numbers of children with special needs, type of accommodation and the policies about grouping of children, and all other factors which may affect the quality of care.

(*b*)   Securing the safety and maintenance of the premises and equipment. This would include fire drills and basic health and safety at work provisions.

(*c*)   Notification of changes in facilities. The Department of Health advises a visit to the premises on receipt of such notification and consideration of any necessary change in requirements and amendments to the certificate of registration.

(*d*)   Specifying the number of persons required to assist. The Department of Health gives detailed advice on the ratios of staff to children and the qualifications/experience required in different settings, normally a ratio of one to three for children under two, one to four for children aged two to three, and one to eight for those aged three to five years for full day care, and a lower ratio for sessional care. These should be treated as the minimum acceptable and may be higher if not all staff are qualified or sufficiently trained. It will be difficult for local authorities to insist on higher staffing ratios in any particular case unless there are special features relating to particular groups of children and their needs. As regards sessional day care 'regular' volunteers and others, even though they may be untrained, may be included in the ratio.

(*e*)   Keeping records of children looked after, persons assisting in looking after such children and persons living or likely to be living on the premises and any changes.

Non-domestic premises – discretionary requirements

Each application will warrant consideration of additional requirements relating to the particular form of activity proposed. Insurance and dietary arrangements and requirements for children with special needs may need to be made explicit. Whatever additional requirements are imposed they must not be incompatible with the mandatory requirements.

Domestic Premises – mandatory requirements

(*a*)   Maximum number of children or maximum number within specified groups. The Department of Health guidance requires a ratio of one to three for children under five, one to six for children aged five to seven, and for children under eight of whom no more than three are under five. Where a childminder has an assistant the same ratios apply for the additional children. In all cases the ratios include the childminder's own children.

The Act permits limiting the numbers, for example, of very young children to be looked after, within the total number permitted. (For

33.9 Registration and Inspection – Day Care

example, three children but no more than one child under two.) In each case the childminders own children should be included in the total number.

(b) Securing the safety and maintenance of the premises and equipment.

(c) Keeping records of children looked after, any assistants or any persons living, or likely at any time to be living at the premises.

(d) Notification of any changes.

Domestic premises – discretionary requirements

Such requirements must not be incompatible with mandatory ones. The Department of Health would like to see local authorities encouraging childminders to take out public liability insurance and considers 'one way of enforcing this might be through a requirement attached to registration'. While that may well be reasonable and prudent, enforcement of failure to comply by cancellation of registration is a draconian step in encouraging carers. Day care policies consulted on, published, and applied to all would seem a necessary preliminary step. Local authorities could also consider negotiating for insurance cover on favourable terms.

Babies and toddlers

Childminding is generally recommended for children under two. Where day care is provided in non-domestic premises additional criteria are suggested by the Department of Health such as separate rooms, staff rotas to ensure as much continuity as possible, each baby to be looked after by one person during each shift, staff awareness of child development in the very young, and ways of identifying at an early stage any adverse effects.

33.9 CANCELLATION OF REGISTRATION

The grounds for cancellation are:

(a) if the circumstances justify refusing to register the person, for example, if evidence is provided that a person is no longer fit to look after children;

(b) the care given to an individual child is seriously inadequate having regard to her/his needs, or having regard to her/his religion, racial origin, cultural or linguistic background;

(c) contravention or failure to comply with any requirement of registration; and

(d) failure to pay the annual inspection fee.

Each of a person's separate registrations may be cancelled where the grounds exist for refusing registration with respect to any premises (for example s/he is not a fit person).

Cancellation must be in writing (see 33.11 APPEALS below). Where the premises are not suitable until repairs or alterations and additions which have been required have been carried out, registration may not be cancelled until any time limit set has expired, and it can be shown that the condition of the premises is due to the required works not having been carried out.

Registration and Inspection – Day Care 33.10

Emergency action

At least 14 days notice of cancellation is required (see 33.11 APPEALS below) and the registered person may then make representation. If the local authority believes that the child who is being looked after or may be looked after, by the childminder or other registered person, is suffering or is likely to suffer significant harm [see *CA 89 s 31(10)*], they may apply to the court for an order cancelling registration, varying any requirement imposed, or removing a requirement, or imposing an additional one. The cancellation, variation etc. has effect from the date on which the order is made.

The application to the court may be made *ex parte* and must be supported by a written statement of the authority's reasons for making it. If the court makes the order the local authority must serve on the registered person, notice of the order and of its terms as soon as reasonably practicable, together with a statement of the authority's reasons in support of their application. Any requirement imposed or varied by the court is treated as having been imposed by the local authority.

Appeal from the making or refusal to make an order cancelling registration under *s* 75 will lie to the High Court but it should be noted that cancellation has effect from the date of the making of the order. If the application is made *ex parte*, there will be an interval before notice is given to the registered person. While there may be reasonable excuse and therefore no offence committed in continuing to provide day care, there will still be a considerable period after notice and before hearing an appeal during which day care cannot be offered. A magistrates' court may grant a stay of execution and it would seem desirable to do so until there has been time to consider the making of an appeal especially if the order is being made *ex parte*. There does not appear to be any other power to delay the effect of the order other than by adjournment before formal pronouncement.

33.10 INSPECTION

Annual inspection

Local authorities must inspect domestic and non-domestic premises at least once every year. Notice of an annual inspection must be given requiring payment of the prescribed fee. It is a condition of continued registration that the fee is paid within 28 days of the date the inspection is carried out. Unnotified inspections of registered premises may be carried out at any reasonable time and there is no limit on the number of such inspections. Where the local authority have reasonable cause to believe that a child is being looked after on any premises in contravention of the Act an authorised person may enter at any reasonable time. For both registered and unregistered day care a power is given to inspect:

(*a*) the premises,

(*b*) any children being looked after on the premises,

(*c*) the arrangements made for their welfare, and

(*d*) any records kept including access to and checking the operation of any computer and associated material. The inspection may require that assistance be given in so doing.

It is an offence to intentionally obstruct anyone exercising the powers of inspection set out above.

33.11 Registration and Inspection – Day Care

Department of Health guidance suggests that there should be a written report of an inspection visit and adequate administrative support for notifications and report writing. Clearly it is prudent to visit premises between initial registration and an annual inspection.

Co-operation between authorities

A local authority may seek the help of any local education authority specifying any action requested. The local education authority is bound to comply if the request is compatible with their own statutory or other duties and obligations and it does not unduly prejudice the discharge of any other functions. This power is useful when dealing with, for example, private nursery schools and services provided for three to four year olds.

33.11 APPEALS

Where a local authority proposes:

(*a*) refusal of an application for registration,

(*b*) cancellation of a registration,

(*c*) refusal of consent to a disqualified person under *Sch 9, para 2*,

(*d*) imposition, removal or variation of a registration requirement, or

(*e*) refusal of an application for variation or removal of a requirement,

at least 14 days notice in writing must be given of the action proposed – 'the step' – giving the authority's reasons for the step and informing the person concerned of her/his rights under *s 77*. If the recipient of the notice then informs the local authority in writing of her/his desire to object, the local authority must give her/him an opportunity to do so. Any objection may be made in person or by a representative. Following consideration of the objection the local authority must give written notice if they nevertheless decide to take the step. A person aggrieved may then appeal against the step to the court. A step, or decision to take a step cancelling registration or imposing, removing or varying a requirement does not take effect, even if there is no appeal, until the time limit for an appeal has elapsed or, if there is an appeal, until its determination. Where the court allows an appeal against refusal or cancellation it may impose requirements under *ss 72 or 73*, and where it allows an appeal against the imposition of a requirement it may vary it. Resulting requirements are then treated as if they have been imposed by the local authority. The advice and assistance of legal departments will be needed not only in respect of court hearings but also in relation to the notice of steps proposed and the hearing of objections.

34 Registration and Inspection – Accommodation

34.1 References

Children Act 1989, Parts VI, VII and VIII
Registered Homes (Amendment) Act 1991
Children's Homes Regulations 1991 (SI 1991 No 1506)
Department of Health guidance Vol 4

34.2 BACKGROUND AND DEFINITIONS

Parts VI, VII and *VIII* of the Act deal respectively with community homes, voluntary homes and registered children's homes to which the *Children's Homes Regulations* apply, creating a code of conduct for the homes as well as registration and inspection. (For the conduct of homes see CONDUCT OF CHILDREN'S HOMES (12).)

Registration of voluntary children's homes was, prior to the Act, the function of the Secretary of State. It remains so, although plans to transfer responsibility to local authorities are under consideration. Private children's homes (now registered children's homes) were also registered by the Secretary of State although the *Children's Homes Act 1982*, never brought into force and now repealed, envisaged regulation by local authorities. This is now brought about by the *Children Act 1989*.

A voluntary home is defined in *s 60* as any home or other institution providing care and accommodation for children which is carried on by a voluntary organisation (a body other than a public or local authority whose activities are not carried on for profit) but does not include nursing, mental nursing or residential care homes, schools, community homes, health service hospitals, homes provided by the Secretary of State, and homes exempted under regulations.

A 'registered children's home' means a home which provides (or usually provides or is intended to provide) care and accommodation wholly and mainly for more than three children at any one time. There are exclusions from this definition. A home is not a children's home for the purposes of registration and inspection as discussed in this chapter if it is any of the following.

(*a*) Exempted under regulations made by the Secretary of State.

(*b*) A voluntary, community, nursing, mental nursing or residential care home (other than a small home under *s 1(4)* of the *Registered Homes (Amendment) Act 1991*).

(N.B. The 1991 Act is likely to be brought into force in the second half of 1992. Homes catering for three or fewer disabled children will then be required to register under the *Registered Homes Act 1984*, unless exempted by regulations to be made under the 1991 Act. The exemption from registration as a children's home will only apply to homes catering for more than three disabled children. Potentially, therefore, these 'small' homes would be liable to register under both Acts. It is anticipated that regulations under either of the Acts will avoid this situation.)

(*c*) A health service hospital.

(*d*) Provided by the Secretary of State.

34.3 Registration and Inspection – Accommodation

(e)   A school (unless providing accommodation for not more than 50 children and not approved by the Secretary of State under *s 11(3)(a)* of the *Education Act 1981*).

Fostering of more than three children

The definition above includes a foster home which normally cares for more than three children as in a number of professional fostering schemes. The Act creates a 'usual' fostering limit of no more than three children excluding siblings which, if exceeded, brings the foster home within the provisions for registration as a children's home. The Act, however, allows the local authority to exempt a foster home from the usual limit (see 23.34 THE USUAL FOSTERING LIMIT). A child is not treated as cared for and accommodated in a children's home if

(a)   s/he is cared for and accommodated by a parent, non-parent with parental responsibility or any relative;

(b)   when any of the above is living at the home; or

(c)   the person caring for her/him is doing so in her/his personal capacity and not in the course of carrying out her/his duties in relation to that home.

34.3   REGISTRATION OF VOLUNTARY HOMES

The form of application and provisions for refusal, cancellation etc. are not dealt with here as they are functions of the Secretary of State. Inspection is dealt with below (see 34.4).

Registration of other children's homes

Homes which comply or will comply with the *Children's Homes Regulations 1991* must be granted registration. This may be conditional or unconditional. The conditions are such as the local authority think fit relating to the conduct of the homes. Conditions may from time to time be varied or new conditions imposed [*s 63* and *Sch 6*]. The local authority is required to carry out an annual review to determine whether registration should continue in force or be cancelled [*Sch 6 para 3* and *SI 1991 No 1506, reg 28*]. This is distinct from 'inspections' dealt with below (see 34.4). The regulations indicate that an inspection should coincide with the annual review [*reg 28(2)*].

Procedure for registration

The person or body proposing to carry on the home must give written notice to the local authority [*reg 25*] for the area in which the home is situated. The local authority may set a reasonable fee. Particulars required with the application are prescribed in *Sch 5* to the regulations. The local authority must inspect the home before making any decision [*reg 28*]. Where the local authority promise to grant the application they must give written notice of any conditions which they will impose, unless these have been agreed, or are those specified in the application itself.

Refusal

Written notice of a proposal to refuse must be given containing the local authority's reasons [*CA Sch 6 paras 5* and *6*] giving 14 days from service [see *s 105(8)*] for the applicant to make representations. No specific grounds for refusal are set out (compare day care in REGISTRATION AND INSPECTION – DAY CARE (33)). The local authority will wish to ensure that the person carrying on the home will be able to comply with the requirements of the regulations regarding conduct of the home, staffing and administration etc. A person disqualified from fostering a child privately (see PRIVATE FOSTERING (31)) is not permitted to carry on or be otherwise concerned with the management of a home or have any financial interest in it unless s/he has disclosed the fact and obtains the consent of the local authority [*s 65*]. Nor may a home employ such person unless similarly the fact has been disclosed and consent obtained. If a local authority refuses consent written notice with reasons must be given and the applicant has a right of appeal to the registered homes tribunal.

The absence of specific grounds highlights the need for the pre-registration visit to consider all aspects of the *Children's Homes Regulations* very carefully so that reasons can be given to justify the decision. Regard should be had to the fitness of the persons carrying on the home, the situation, construction, state of repair, accommodation, staffing and equipment of the premises, and the provision of services or facilities reasonably required. Guidance on staffing, accommodation standards etc. can be taken from the regulations themselves and the associated Department of Health guidance.

Conditions of registration

The local authority may impose 'such conditions as they think fit' and from time to time vary any conditions or impose additional ones either on application by the person carrying on the home or of its own motion. Notice must be given of such a proposal by the local authority and representations may be made as above. The regulations provide [*reg 26*] specifically for the local authority to set a limit on the number of children to be accommodated [*CA Sch 6*].

Representations

These may be made orally or in writing. If made orally the local authority must give the person an opportunity of appearing before a committee or sub-committee [*Sch 6 paras 5* and *6*]. Unlike *s 77* (objection to a 'step' – 33.10 INSPECTION above) the regulations do not provide for the representations to be made 'in person or by a representative'. The making of representations is not an appeal, as the representations are about a proposal (see Registered Homes Tribunal Decision No 7 for the procedure to be adopted).

Cancellation of registration

The home itself may apply for cancellation [*Sch 6 para 4*]. A school registered under *s 63(6)* must be deregistered if that section no longer applies (see SCHOOLS (39)). If at the time of annual review or at any other time it appears to the local authority that a registered home is being carried on otherwise than in accordance with the relevant requirements they may cancel the registration. Relevant requirements mean those prescribed under the regulations and such conditions as have been imposed.

34.4 Registration and Inspection – Accommodation

Appeals

The decision of a local authority, other than in granting an application with agreed conditions, does not take effect until 28 days after service of notice of the decision. If an appeal is brought to the registered homes tribunal it must be made within 28 days of the notice and written notification given to the local authority. The tribunal has power [*Sch 6 para 8*] to uphold or overturn the local authority's decision and to vary or revoke any condition in force or impose a new one. No fresh application for registration may be made within six months of refusal by the local authority or determination by the tribunal, nor where the registration of a home is cancelled.

34.4 INSPECTION OF AND VISITS TO VOLUNTARY AND REGISTERED CHILDREN'S HOMES

Duties of local authorities

Every local authority must satisfy themselves that any voluntary organisation or registered home, within its area or providing accommodation outside its area on behalf of that local authority, are 'satisfactorily safeguarding and promoting the welfare of children so accommodated' [*ss 62(1)* and *64(4)*]. Every local authority must arrange for children accommodated within their area to be visited from time to time in the interests of their welfare. If the local authority are not satisfied that the child's welfare is being satisfactorily safeguarded or promoted they must take all reasonably practicable steps to ensure that care and accommodation is undertaken by a parent, non-parent with parental responsibility, or a relative and consider the extent to which (if at all) they should exercise any of their functions with respect to the child.

Any person authorised by the local authority may, in order to discharge their duties, enter at any reasonable time and inspect any homes, premises, inspect any children and examine any records required by the regulations (including access to computerised records). Intentional obstruction of the inspection is an offence.

Children's homes regulations

The Act does not lay down any annual review procedure in respect of voluntary homes as it does for the registered children's homes. However, the regulations require the voluntary home to make an annual return to the Secretary of State.

Inspection of registered children's homes

Apart from the duties and powers to enter and inspect set out above, the homes must be inspected before registration and also on the occasion of the annual review (see 34.3 REGISTRATION OF VOLUNTARY HOMES above). *Regulation 31(3)* also requires that the home be inspected on at least one other occasion in any year. These two inspections can be regarded as the minimum required to comply with the local authority's duties under *ss 62* and *64*. Notice of an annual inspection may be given to the home but must not be given in respect of any other inspection. Reports of inspections must be considered by the local authority when determining whether or not the registration should be reviewed or cancelled. It would be good practice for copies of the report to be supplied to the persons responsible for the home. Acceptance of the report may be useful evidence in any subsequent proceedings.

Registration and Inspection – Accommodation 34.4

Inspection of voluntary homes

The regulations do not lay down any requirements for inspection and the Act itself is the basis for inspection 'at will' as part of the local authority's duties to safeguard and promote the welfare of children accommodated.

Visits by the local authority to voluntary and registered children's homes

The regulations distinguish between inspections and visits. Visits are required in specified circumstances [*reg 34*] over and above the visits required by the Act as set out above:

(a) within ninety days of notification of the placement of a child in the care of another local authority or within twenty-eight days of notification of placement of any other child;

(b) within fourteen days of representations by the home that the circumstances of any child require a visit; and

(c) within seven days of being informed that the welfare of a child may not be satisfactorily safeguarded or promoted.

Further visits must be arranged suitable to the particular circumstances, but in any event

(i) within twelve months of the first visit to a child as a result of notice being given of her/his placement by another local authority, if the first visit proves satisfactory; and

(ii) within six months of the first visit to a child notified as placed by a voluntary organisation; or

(iii) where the local authority is not satisfied on the first visit but allow the child to continue to live in the home, within 28 days.

Seeing the child

During the course of any required visit the local authority must see the child unless, exceptionally, the officer thinks it unnecessary. The local authority must also

(a) read all relevant case papers and records and sign and date them to indicate s/he has seen them;

(b) make a written report which shall be made available to all relevant inspectors (this presumably includes inspectors in other local authorities) and copied to the child's care authority and to the persons carrying on the home. The home must provide 'suitable accommodation' for the visit.

Further action

Where the officer of the local authority is not satisfied as regards the welfare of a child in the care of another local authority, the officer's local authority must notify that other local authority within 14 days of the reasons for concern and that they will consider placing with a parent, relative or using other powers within a further 14 days unless satisfied that the child's welfare is being safeguarded and promoted [*regs 32* and *33*].

34.4 Registration and Inspection – Accommodation

Inspection of other homes and schools – *ss 85 to 87*

Consistent with the aim of securing the welfare of children irrespective of the type of placement, the Act has brought health and education authorities and homes registered under the *Registered Homes Act 1984* within the ambit of local authority powers to safeguard and promote welfare [*ss 85 to 87*]. The appropriate local authority must be notified of the placement and discharge of children accommodated for a consecutive period of three months or whom it is intended will be so accommodated by any health or education authority or home governed by the *Registered Homes Act 1984*. The placement of children in independent schools does not require notification but the local authority has duties in respect of children accommodated there (see SCHOOLS (39) below).

The responsible authority in respect of health and education authority accommodation is the local authority for the area in which the child was ordinarily resident immediately before placement, or if no ordinary residence is established the local authority for the area in which the accommodation is situated. In the case of a home governed by the *Registered Homes Act 1984*, a person carrying on the home must notify the local authority for the area in which the home is situated. In determining ordinary residence, no regard is to be had to any period in which a child lived in any place:

(*a*)   which is a school, or other institution;

(*b*)   while under a supervision order with a residence requirement;

(*c*)   while accommodated by or on behalf of a local authority [*s 105(6)*].

Local authority powers and duties

Where a local authority is notified of the placement of a child in their area they are under a duty [*ss 85(4) and 86(3)*] to:

(*a*)   take such steps as are reasonably practicable to enable them to determine whether the child's welfare is adequately safeguarded and promoted; and

(*b*)   consider the extent to which, if at all, they should exercise any of their functions with regard to the child.

The duty is onerous involving what may be considerable time and travelling for local authority staff and expense in meeting any demands for the exercise of any of their functions. This may, for example, include assistance to parents to maintain contact, and the provision of ancillary services to the home or institution which may be necessary to meet special needs. The wording of the sections allow for arrangements between local authorities for duties to be carried out by the authority for the area in which the home is situated, but even this may give rise to charges for services rendered. Department of Health guidance suggests that initial contact regarding the child could be made with the health and education authority or home within 14 days and that this could be by letter or phone. The main concern in the guidance is regarding parental contact, however, as the nature of the accommodation may not be known to the responsible local authority and information on the circumstances of each child will be required. Such enquiries may be a little too cursory. The guidance suggests that any concern should be taken care of by arrangements to visit the child not later than 14 days from the concerns arising.

The qualifying period of a consecutive period of three months will rule out a number of educational establishments where children come home for school holidays.

Registered Homes Act 1984

Homes may be entered and visited by persons authorised by the local authority, to establish whether the requirements of *s 86* are being met and the Act creates an offence of intentional obstruction of such entry. Co-operation between social services departments and health and education authorities obviates the need for such provisions as regards accommodation provided by them.

Independent schools

Independent schools providing accommodation for not more than 50 children and not approved under *s 11(3)(a)* of the *Education Act 1981* are children's homes requiring registration by the local authority [*CA 89 s 63(6)*]. The local authority for the area in which an independent school, which is not registered as a children's or residential care home, is situated has a duty to take reasonably practicable steps to determine whether the child's welfare is adequately safeguarded and promoted and if not so satisfied, to notify the Secretary of State. A person authorised by the local authority may enter any independent school in their area at any reasonable time to discharge that duty and may carry out inspections of premises, children and records [*CA 89 s 87(5)* and *Inspection of Premises, Children and Records (Independent Schools) Regulations 1991 (SI 1991 No 975)*].

35 Remands

35.1 **References**

Children and Young Persons Act 1969, s 23 (as amended by *CA Sch 12, paras 26* and *29*)

35.2 The law relating to remands has been changed to the extent that the remand of a child (unless s/he is certified unruly or is bailed) is no longer to the care of a local authority but to 'local authority accommodation'. It is difficult to determine whether any substantive changes in the law have been affected by this. Local authority accommodation is defined in the 1969 Act (as amended by *Sch 12, para 29*) as 'accommodation provided by or on behalf of a local authority (within the meaning of the *Children Act 1989*)'. A child so remanded is 'looked after' by the local authority as the accommodation is provided in the exercise of functions which stand referred to the social services committee [*s 22(1)(b)*]. By *s 23* of the 1989 Act the authority's duty is to provide accommodation for a child looked after in a number of ways set out in *s 23(2)*, and this includes 'foster placement' and a placement with her/his own parents. As the child is not in care the authority has in fact a duty to place with parents etc. under *s 23(6)* subject to regulations made under that subsection (none have so far been made). It would seem strange that *s 23* has not been simply amended by the substitution of 'to local authority accommodation' for 'to the care of a local authority' if the intention was to remove local authority discretion to allow the child to live at home. However the effect of the amended section is that the child must be placed at home or with a relative, friend or other person connected with her/him unless that would not be reasonably practicable or consistent with her/his welfare [*s 23(6)*]. A further effect is that the authority has a duty to ascertain the wishes and feelings of the child and others and give due consideration to them [*s 22(4)*].

35.3 The *Placement of Children Regulations* would seem quite inappropriate for remands but nevertheless the definition of placement would encompass the provision of such accommodation – 'provision of accommodation and maintenance by a local authority for any child whom they are looking after . . .'.

There would appear to be a contrary intention in the wording of *s 21(2)(c)(1)* which requires a designated authority to 'receive and provide accommodation for children on remand under section 23(1) of the Children and Young Persons Act 1969'. The difficulty in interpreting the 1989 Act lies in the definition of 'looking after' as accommodation provided in the exercise of functions which are referred to a social services committee still includes that specified under *s 23* of *CYPA 1969*. While the amended *s 23* of *CYPA 1969* makes it lawful for any person acting on behalf of the authority to detain a child remanded to local authority accommodation it does not insist that a child be in fact detained by them.

35.4 There is no qualification as to remands (similar to the power of a court imposing a residence requirement under a supervision order [*CYPA 1969, s 12*] which also requires a child to live for a specified period in local authority accommodation) to stipulate that a child shall not live with a named person. The apparent necessity to include such a power confirms the view that an authority may, if not must, place a child remanded with parents etc. Unless, therefore, the authority take the view on 'welfare' not to place, there is nothing to be gained from a remand to local authority accommodation over a remand on bail. The position under previous legislation remains, but subject to duties and regulations which are inappropriate and require, first consideration to be given to placement at home which must be inconsistent with a court's decision to remand other than on bail. There is further confirmation that a child on remand is 'looked after' when accommodated by a local authority in the *Children (Secure Accommodation) Regulations 1991 (SI 1991 No 1505), reg 6* (see SECURE ACCOMMODATION (42)) which modifies *s 25* in relation to children who are being looked after by a local authority and are 'children remanded to local authority accommodation under section 23 of the Children and Young Persons Act 1969 . . .'.

36 Reports to the Court

36.1 **References**

Children Act 1989, s 7
Family Proceedings Courts (Children Act 1989) Rules 1991 (SI 1991 No 1395)
Family Proceedings Rules 1991 (SI 1991 No 1247)

36.2 A court considering any question with respect to a child under the 1989 Act may request a report from a probation officer or officer of a local authority (the welfare officer). That officer has a duty to comply with the request.

36.3 The court rules [*SI 1991 No 1395 r 17* and *SI 1991 No 1247 r 4(17)*] require that parties serve on the welfare officer copies of documents and statements of the substance of oral evidence which they intend to adduce.

36.4 The welfare report must be filed when directed by the court or at the least five days before a hearing at which the report will be considered. The officer must then attend unless excused, and may be questioned by the parties.

36.5 The report may be made in writing or orally as the court directs and 'hearsay' statements may be taken account of by the court if considered relevant [*CA 89 s 7*].

37 Respite Care

37.1 **References**

Children Act 1989, ss 17(1) and *22(1)(b)*
National Health Service Act 1977, Sch 8
Local Authority Social Services Act 1970
Arrangements for Placement of Children (General) Regulations 1991 (SI 1991 No 890)

37.2 Local authorities are under a duty to provide a full range of services for children who are in need [*s 17(1)*] (see SUPPORT FOR FAMILIES AND CHILDREN (44)). Further powers are available under, for example, *Sch 8* of the *National Health Service Act 1977*. The ability to provide respite care has not been limited in any way by *CA 89*, but it does require that all children in need are dealt with in the same way, irrespective of the reason they are in need and the type of placement made. Respite care will attract all the duties and safeguards set out in the Act and regulations e.g. inspection, promotion of welfare etc. If accommodation is provided by the authority in the exercise of any functions referred to the social services committee under the *Local Authority Social Services Act 1970 (LASSA)* then the child is being 'looked after' [*CA 89 s 22(1)(b)*] (functions under *Sch 8* of the 1977 Act stand referred to social services committees). Placement of children looked after by a local authority is governed by the *Arrangements for Placement of Children (General) Regulations 1991* (see FOSTER PARENTS (23)).

37.3 *Regulation 13* deals with application of the regulations to short-term placements. Any series of short-term (respite) placements at the same place may be treated as a single placement provided:

(i) all the placements occur within one year;

(ii) no single placement exceeds four weeks; and

(iii) the total duration does not exceed ninety days.

A written plan will still be necessary as the regulations for a single placement must be followed.

38 Reviews

38.1 References

Children Act 1989, s 26
Review of Children's Cases Regulations 1991 (SI 1991 No 895)

38.2 INTRODUCTION

The Act and regulations create a system for reviews of children's cases that is more carefully prescribed than in previous legislation. Hitherto, the frequency of reviews, but not their content or procedure was the only topic covered by law, although provision for the type of regulations now in force had been made in *s 20* of the *Child Care Act 1980* but never implemented. The matters dealt with below are, then, totally new legislative requirements although they may indeed reflect some of the practice of authorities.

38.3 SUMMARY OF REQUIREMENTS

Application. Any child being looked after or accommodated by a local authority, a voluntary organisation or in a registered children's home.

Responsible authority. Local authority, voluntary organisation or registered children's home.

Timing. First review – within four weeks of the date when the child accommodated. Subsequently not later than three months from the first review and six months thereafter.

Procedure.

— Arrangements to be in writing and drawn to the attention of persons to be consulted.

— Arrangements to be monitored.

— Consultation, participation and notification prescribed.

— All aspects of the review to be co-ordinated with the assistance of a specially designated officer.

— Review information to be recorded in writing.

Content. Prescribed in *Schs 1, 2* and *3* of *SI 1991 No 895* to include providing relevant information to participants, possible changes in arrangements, consideration of contact, education and health care.

Health review. Written assessment of health and need for health care six-monthly up to the age of two and then annually.

Short periods of care. Up to the total of ninety days duration to be treated as one episode.

38.4 The regulations apply to children being looked after 'or provided with accommodation'. The latter words are necessary to include children provided with accommodation by a voluntary organisation otherwise than on behalf of a local authority, or accommodated in a registered children's home otherwise than on behalf of a local authority.

A child in care or provided with accommodation, no matter where, by a local authority in the exercise of any functions referred to the Social Services Committee is covered by the regulations, so that, for example, accommodation in a mental nursing home does not obviate the need to review. The review of a child placed in secure accommodation (see SECURE ACCOMMODATION (42)) will be in addition to the reviews under *s 26*.

38.5 The body responsible for holding the review is the local authority if the child is being looked after by them, or, if not accommodated on behalf of a local authority, the voluntary organisation or person carrying on a registered children's home which is providing accommodation.

38.6 WHAT CONSTITUTES A REVIEW?

According to the Department of Health guidance (Vol 3 Family Placements): 'Any meeting which is convened for the purpose of considering the child's case in connection with any aspect of the review of that case falls within the scope of the Regulations . . .', and also 'But where the discussion at a case conference comprises consideration of wider issues affecting the plan for the child, it constitutes part of a review and falls within these regulations'.

As indicated below, there will be necessary preparations for the review including meetings of e.g. local authority staff. Such preparation need not constitute a review meeting which requires, for example, consideration of parental attendance.

38.7 Timing

Regulation 3 sets out the maximum intervals between reviews. As indicated above, more frequent reviews may be desirable and arranged either at the instigation of the responsible authority or the parents.

38.8 Short-term placements

Clearly arrangements for short periods of 'respite care', for example, could require separate reviews for each period if the regulations did not (as with the *Arrangements for Placement of Children (General) Regulations 1991 (SI 1991 No 890)*) make specific provision otherwise. Provided all the short-term placements are within a period which does not exceed one year and at the same place then single periods of up to four weeks amounting to no more than ninety days in the year are treated as one placement. As placements of more than one week in four within a year are not within the definition of 'short periods' each placement would attract the review requirements in full (in parallel with the *Arrangements for Placement of Children Regulations*).

38.9 Procedure

The child, her/his parents, non-parent with parental responsibility and any other person whose views the responsible authority consider relevant must be informed of the written arrangements made for the conduct of reviews.

38.10 Reviews

Guardians *ad litem* are authorised to inspect and take copies of all records relating to the child held by a local authority (or authorised person), compiled in connection with their social services functions which could include any written records required by these regulations. That would not, however, include the written arrangements for the conduct of the review. GALs may nevertheless wish to comment on any report to the court on the system for involving parents and others in the review process.

The monitoring of the procedure should be concerned with all aspects, and not merely the adherence to timetables.

It is important to be clear as to the meaning of 'any meeting which is to consider the child's case in connection with any aspect of the review of that case' at which the regulations require the authority to consider, for example, the attendance of parents and child. The DOH guidance excludes case discussions, case conferences (unless it combines consideration of wider issues affecting the plan for the child) and case reviews under *Working Together* (Guidance Part 7). 'Any aspect of the review' covers a multitude of issues set out in three Schedules to the regulations (see 38.15 CONTENT OF REVIEW below). It would be awesome to act on the basis that any meeting to formulate proposals for discussion with parents etc. calls for anything other than the normal case file recording that a local authority would undertake as a matter of practice. While it is right therefore to see reviews as part of a continuing planning process, any changes proposed to the plan for a child as a result, for example, of the wider deliberations of a case conference, would be covered as regards local authorities by $s\ 22(4)(5)$ which also deals with prior consultation. Options and case discussion may shade into planning for the child's future which would require parental involvement but in this respect perhaps it is best to take the guidance as demonstrating enthusiasm for participation/consultation and indeed its necessity if the Act is to live up to its good intentions. Involvement by attendance at meetings may not always be appropriate or desirable.

The suggestion that discussion at a case conference could fall within the scope of the regulations is misconceived. If there are changes in the plan for the child arising from, for example, a case conference, they will become matters considered in the review and for possible change in the written arrangements for the child's placement. It is important to note that a written record is required of the proceedings at any meeting arranged by the responsible authority at which the child's case is considered in connection with any aspect of the review of that case. Although a case conference is not such a meeting it is unlikely that the conference will not be minuted. Parental attendance at case conferences is virtually demanded as a result of the advice in *Working Together* and in practice any difficulties in interpretation should be resolved if the relevant parties are kept informed of the authorities views.

38.10 Consultation

Quite apart from the duty [*ss 22(4), 61* and *64*] to take account of the wishes and feelings of the child and others before making any decision, the regulations impose their own duty to consult by seeking and taking into account the views of all relevant persons before conducting the review (unless not reasonably practicable). This is in accord with the tenor of EC legislation (see CONSULTATION/PARTICIPATION (11)) as well as good practice. Case file records as well as any written information accumulated for the purposes of the review should document the results of consultation.

38.11 Participation

The child's parents etc. must be involved including attending where the authority consider it appropriate. The guidance expects that 'attendance of the child and his parents at meetings to review the child's case will be the norm rather than the exception'. Procedures should make clear any reasons considered valid for non-attendance or partial participation – this aspect of reviews should also be carefully monitored. The authority will have in this connection to consider the venue e.g. payment of expenses if attendance is to be encouraged and also the possibility of advocacy for the child. The DOH suggests that exclusion from the whole or part of a meeting should be discussed and agreed with the chairperson and a written explanation given to the parents, with a copy placed on the child's record and other arrangements made for their involvement in the review. The list of potential invitees will stretch from the child's carer to 'ethnic minority representative' and cannot be exhaustively defined. Social work and administrative resources will undoubtedly restrict the contacts made between reviews although the planning and review process set out in the Act and regulations looks to the ideal in practice.

38.12 Notification

Details of the result of the review and any decision taken in consequence must be given in writing [*regs 1(3)* and *7*] to all those required to be consulted. A copy of the review report [*reg 10*] including all written views communicated would be appropriate, although it may be necessary to take particular care in dealing with confidential health information. DOH guidance suggests a written summary of the main points of the report of the review making clear who is responsible for action and explanation in person to those not present within 14 days.

38.13 Co-ordination

Officers to co-ordinate the carrying out of reviews must be designated [*reg 4(3)*]. As pointed out above there will be a considerable administrative burden in addition to social work considerations. Choosing the right time and place will not be an easy task and such a designation would seem to be inevitable regardless of the regulations.

38.14 Written review report

A written record is required which must be placed on the child's case record [*reg 10*]. It may be desirable for the report to go to others (e.g foster care unit's social worker). All information obtained for the review, details of the proceedings at any meeting arranged and details of any decisions must be included in the report. A minute of any meeting 'in connection with any aspect of the review' should already have been prepared and clearly the regulations envisage a comprehensive record which would serve the requirement to monitor fully a child's progress whilst accommodated and the fulfilment of statutory and departmental policy requirements. There is an obvious implication for the other recordings on a child's case file.

38.15 Content of review – *Schedules 1, 2* and *3*

The elements to be included and considerations to which the responsible authorities must have regard are set out in the three Schedules to the

38.15 Reviews

regulations. *Schedule 3* deals specifically with health considerations. This points to the need to obtain written reports, at the least from GPs, health visitors etc. and consider any preventive measures that may be required. Apart from the obvious review of arrangements for contact, specific attention must be paid to the possibility of a change in the child's legal status (whether by discharge of a care order or otherwise), educational needs, after care and permanent substitute family placement, and the appointment of an independent visitor (see INDEPENDENT VISITOR (26)). Health considerations included in the review under *Sch 3* are separate from other requirements of the regulations to conduct health reviews [*reg 6*]. The responsible authority must arrange for examination and a written assessment on the child's state of health, and need for health care at least six-monthly up to the child's second birthday, and at least annually thereafter. [*Schs 1, 2* and *3*].

39 Schools

39.1 **References**

Children Act 1989, ss 61, 63, 64 and *87*
Registered Homes Act 1984
Inspection of Premises Children and Records (Independent Schools) Regulations 1991 (SI 1991 No 975)

39.2 With the exception of those schools dealt with in 39.3 below, the proprietors of independent schools providing accommodation for any child are responsible for safeguarding and promoting the child's welfare.

Local authorities have a duty under *CA 89, s 87* to take reasonably practicable steps to determine whether this has been achieved. Any failure must be notified to the Secretary of State. Periodic visits are required and the regulations allow inspection of the children individually or collectively (medical examinations are subject to the child's consent if s/he is of sufficient understanding to give or withhold consent). Premises and certain records may also be inspected.

39.3 **SCHOOLS WHICH ARE CHILDREN'S HOMES, RESIDENTIAL CARE HOMES OR NON-MAINTAINED SPECIAL SCHOOLS**

Schools with 50 or fewer children in residential accommodation and not approved by the local education authority for the placement of children with statements of special educational needs are children's homes and require registration as such (see REGISTRATION AND INSPECTION – CHILDREN'S HOMES AND OTHER ACCOMMODATION (34)).

Schools with 50 or fewer children in residential accommodation and not approved under the *Education Act 1981* may be required to register as residential care homes under the *Registered Homes Act 1984* as providing personal care for children who are disabled or mentally disordered. Some independent schools which would otherwise by virtue of the above be treated as children's homes may nevertheless, if more than four children are accommodated, be required to register as residential care homes.

A non-maintained special school provided by a voluntary organisation is not an independent school, but by *s 61* its organisation has a duty to safeguard and promote the welfare of children accommodated by or on their behalf.

Accommodation can be within the school or by arrangements made by the school, for example, with landladies. The duties remain with the proprietor unless the accommodation is a private fostering or otherwise clearly not arranged by the school.

40 Secretary of State's Powers

40.1 References
Children Act 1989, ss 80–84

40.2 BACKGROUND
The 'default' powers of the Secretary of State [*s 84*] are dealt with in CONSULTATION/PARTICIPATION (11). Apart from the numerous powers to make regulations under the Act, the Secretary of State's supervisory functions and responsibilities contained in the *Child Care Act 1980* have been repealed and re-enacted with some modifications in *Part XI* of the *Children Act 1989*.

40.3 INSPECTION
The Secretary of State has power to inspect certain premises, children living there, records, and to require information. The premises include day care, residential and other accommodation including private foster homes and the homes of prospective adopters [*s 80*].

40.4 INQUIRIES
The Secretary of State's power to order an inquiry has been widened to include any matter connected with a registered children's home and a residential care, nursing or mental nursing home. These are in addition to powers under previous legislation to inquire into the functions of social services committees, adoption agencies, voluntary organisations and youth treatment centres. An enquiry may sit in private at the direction of the Secretary of State or at the instance of the person holding the inquiry. Such inquiries, unlike those initiated by a local authority, are able to subpoena witnesses, take evidence under oath and make orders as to costs [*s 81*].

40.5 FINANCIAL SUPPORT
Grants towards the cost of training and secure accommodation are dealt with in *s 82* which also enables youth treatment centres to be maintained by the Secretary of State [*s 82*].

40.6 RESEARCH AND RETURNS OF INFORMATION
The provisions for research and returns of information in *s 83* are virtually re-enactments of previous legislation with the exception that a voluntary organisation may now be required to submit returns of children accommodated by them or on their behalf [*s 83*].

41 Section 8 Orders

41.1 References

Children Act 1989, ss 8 and *11*
Family Proceedings Rules (SI 1991 No 1247)
Family Proceedings Courts (Children Act 1989) Rules (SI 1991 No 1395)

41.2 INTRODUCTION

Section 8 of the Act specifies four types of order that the court can make in relation to children. A contact order, a prohibited steps order, a residence order and a specific issue order. These have already become known as *s 8* orders. Each of the orders is dealt with separately below but there are general points that apply to all of them.

In the first place, before making any of these orders, the court must make the child's welfare its first consideration [*s 1(1)*]. The court must not make an order unless it considers that to do so would be better for the child than making no order at all [*s 1(5)*].

Where an application to make, vary or discharge a *s 8* order is opposed then the court must have regard to the welfare check list set out in *s 1(3)* of the Act. This does not apply where an application to make, vary or discharge a *s 8* order is not opposed.

The timetabling provisions and the general principle against delay [*CA 89 s 11*] apply to *s 8* applications in the same way as they do to other proceedings under the Act.

Section 8 orders can be made in other family proceedings (see FAMILY PROCEEDINGS (22)). This means that in an application for an adoption order the court has the power to make a *s 8* order instead. This might mean, for example, that instead of making an adoption order the court might make a residence order in favour of the prospective adopters and in appropriate cases a contact order in respect of other family members.

41.3 INTERIM ORDERS

Where an application has been made to the court for a *s 8* order or to vary or discharge one, the court has the power to make an order before the proceedings even though it is not in a position to finally dispose of the proceedings [*s 11(3)*].

41.4 DIRECTIONS AND CONDITIONS

Section 8 orders may also contain directions about how they are to be carried into effect and impose conditions on anyone in whose favour the order is made or who is a parent or who has parental responsibility or is the person with whom the child is living [*s 11(7)*].

41.5 Section 8 Orders

41.5 LENGTH OF ORDERS

Section 8 orders can be made to last for a specific period of time or to contain conditions or terms which are to have effect for a specified period of time and can include such additional provisions as the court thinks fit [*s 11(7)*]. *Section 8* orders can only be made in respect of children aged 16 or over if the court is satisfied that the circumstances of the case are exceptional. Otherwise orders should not be made to last after the child is 16 unless there are exceptional circumstances [*s 9(6)* and *(7)*].

41.6 WHO CAN APPLY

Application for s 8 orders

Local authorities cannot apply for residence or contact orders, nor can such orders be made in their favour [*s 9(2)*]. Children who are being looked after by local authorities will either be looked after in accordance with the provisions of *Part III* of the Act (see SUPPORT FOR FAMILIES AND CHILDREN (44)) or as a result of a care order being made (see CARE AND SUPERVISION ORDERS (3)).

A court cannot make any *s 8* order except a residence order in relation to a child who is in the care of the local authority.

The Act provides for two categories of person who can apply for *s 8* orders: those who can apply as of right and those who can apply with the leave of the court.

Those entitled to apply as of right for any *s 8* order [see *s 10(4)*]:

— parents, including unmarried fathers, guardians and those with a residence order in their favour.

Those entitled to apply for a residence or contact order [see *s 10(5)*]:

— parties to a marriage, whether or not it is still subsisting, where the child is a child of the family;

— anyone with whom the child has lived for a period of at least three years. This does not have to be continuous but must not have begun more than five years before or ended more than three months before the application was made;

— anyone who has the consent of those in whose favour a residence order is in force;

— the local authority if the child is in the care of the local authority; or

— those who have parental responsibility for the child.

41.7 Applying for leave

Anyone else must apply for leave. A child can apply for leave to apply for a *s 8* order but the court should only grant leave if satisfied that the child has sufficient understanding to make the application for the order [*s 10(8)*]. Where the application for leave is made by someone other than the child, the court should, when deciding whether or not to grant leave, have particular regard to:

— the nature of the proposed application for a *s 8* order;

— the applicant's connection with the child;

— any risk there might be that the proposed application might disrupt the child's life to such an extent that the child might be harmed by it; and

— where the child is being looked after by a local authority the authority's plans for the child's future and the wishes and feelings of the child's parents [s 10(9)].

41.8 **Restrictions on local authority foster parents**

It is important to note that anyone who is or was at any time during the last six months a local authority foster parent of a child cannot apply for leave to apply for a residence or contact order in relation to that child unless

— they are a relative of the child [see s 105];

— the child has been living with them for at least three years; or

— the local authority consents [s 9(3)].

Otherwise anyone can apply for leave to apply for a s 8 order although local authorities cannot apply for any s 8 orders other than specific issue orders and prohibited steps orders [s 9(2)].

If a court makes a residence order in relation to a child who is in the care of the local authority, the care order is discharged [s 91(1)] and if a court makes a care order in respect of a child who is the subject of a s 8 order, that s 8 order is discharged [s 91(2)]. These provisions mean that the courts cannot use s 8 orders to fetter the local authorities discretion in relation to children who are in their care in the way that that discretion could be circumscribed before in wardship proceedings, for example. Contact orders relating to children in care are dealt with in CA 89, s 34 (see CONTACT (13)).

41.9 **RESIDENCE ORDERS**

A residence order means an order settling the arrangements to be made as to the person with whom a child is to live [s 8(1)]. It is similar to, but not the same as, a custody order under the old legislation. A parent does not lose parental responsibility because a residence order is made in respect of another parent or somebody else.

Although the Act says that a residence order settles the arrangements as to the 'person' with whom the child is to live, it presumes that the singular includes the plural [see the *Interpretation Act 1978, s 6*]. This means that residence orders can be made in favour of more than one person. For example, a residence order could be made in favour of a parent and step-parent. This might happen where a parent and step-parent wish to adopt a child but the court feels that in the circumstances of the case a joint residence order would be more appropriate. This is likely to happen where the child's natural father still has contact with the child.

Residence orders can be made to cover the position where the care of the child is shared between parents because s 11(4) states that where a residence order is made in favour of two or more persons who do not themselves all live together, the order may specify the periods during which the child is to live in the different households concerned.

A residence order confers parental responsibility on the person in whose favour it is made [s 12] (see PARENTAL RESPONSIBILITY (28)).

41.10 Section 8 Orders

Where a residence order provides that the child lives, or is to live with one of two parents who each have parental responsibility for the child, the order will cease to have effect if the parents live together for a continuous period of more than six months [see *s 11(5)*].

41.10 CONTACT ORDERS

A contact order is defined in the Act as meaning

> 'an order requiring the person with whom the child lives, or is to live, to allow the child to visit or stay with the person named in the order or for that person and the child otherwise to have contact with each other' [*s 8*].

Contact orders replace but are not exactly equivalent to orders for access made under the old legislation. They will normally be made where there is a dispute between the parents of a child as to the arrangements for contact. They are not, however, limited to this since they can be made in relation to people who are not parents, for example grandparents and others can, with the court's leave, apply for contact orders (see 41.6 above). There can also be more than one contact order in relation to any child, dealing with the contact the child is to have with different people.

The word 'contact' and the way in which the order is described in the Act make it clear that it is not limited to physical contact but can include other forms of contact, for example letters and telephone calls. A contact order may also define contact for long or short periods of time. A contact order is intended to be seen as a positive order and should not therefore be used to prohibit contact. That end, where necessary, will be achieved either by making no order at all or by making a prohibited steps order (see 41.11 below).

41.11 A SPECIFIC ISSUE ORDER AND A PROHIBITED STEPS ORDER

A 'specific issue order' is defined in the Act as

> 'an order giving directions for the purpose of determining a specific question which has arisen or might arise, in connection with any aspect of parental responsibility for a child'.

A prohibited steps order is defined in the Act as

> 'an order that no step which could be taken by a parent in meeting his parental responsibility for a child, and which is of a kind specified in the order, shall be taken by any person without the consent of the court'

[*s 8*].

These two orders give the courts the power to make specific orders in relation to a wide variety of issues concerning the child's life. However, both prohibited steps and specific issue orders may only be made in relation to aspects of parental responsibility. That means, for example, that a court could not order a local authority to make a specific issue order requiring the authority to provide services. It may also be the case that the court will not feel able to make a prohibited steps order preventing a parent from hitting a child if the view is taken that striking children is not an exercise of parental responsibility. The ways in which it is likely that prohibited steps orders will most commonly be used are in cases where it is sought to prevent a parent either having contact with her/his child or from taking the child out of the country.

Section 8 Orders 41.11

Specific issue orders are likely to be used where there is a dispute as to the child's education or as to what medical treatment, if any, the child receives.

However, the Act specifies that neither a prohibited steps order nor a specific issue order should be made with a view to achieving a result which could be achieved by a residence or contact order [*s 9(5)*]. Nor should specific issue orders or prohibited steps orders be used by local authorities to achieve the same effect as a care or supervision order or for them to obtain an order that the child be accommodated by them or that they acquire any aspect of parental responsibility [*s 9(5)*]. It follows from this that a prohibited steps order could not be made preventing a parent removing the child from accommodation provided by a local authority.

42 Secure Accommodation

42.1 References

Children Act 1989, ss 20(8), 25 and *Sch 2, para 7(c)*
Children (Secure Accommodation) Regulations 1991 (SI 1991 No 1505)
Children (Secure Accommodation (No 2) Regulations 1991 SI 1991 No 2034)
Department of Health guidance Vol 4 Ch 8

42.2 DEFINITIONS

Secure accommodation is accommodation provided for the purpose of restricting the liberty of children to whom *s 25* applies. Such accommodation may be provided not only in community homes but (when regulations are made) by health authorities, local education authorities, national health service trusts or in residential care, nursing or mental nursing homes. The regulations prohibit, however, the use of accommodation for the purpose of restricting liberty in voluntary and registered children's homes [*reg 18 SI 1991 No 1505*].

42.3 CHILD TO WHOM SECTION 25 APPLIES

Section 25 applies to children looked after by local authorities [*CA 89 s 22*] and also in a limited way to children accommodated by health and education authorities, National Health Service trusts, and in residential care nursing or mental nursing homes. The section also applies with modifications to children detained and remanded (see 42.8 below).

However *s 25* does not apply to a child

(a) detained under any provision of the *Mental Health Act 1983*;

(b) under *s 53* of the *CYPA 1933*;

(c) over 16, accommodated in a community home under *s 20(5)*; or

(d) kept away from home pursuant to a child assessment order.

[*Regs 5, 6* and *7, SI 1991 No 1505*].

42.4 Special cases

Children under 13 may not be placed in secure accommodation without prior approval of the Secretary of State [*reg 4*].

42.5 The accommodation

A community home can only be used if it has been approved by the Secretary of State (subject to any terms and conditions imposed).

42.6 Avoiding placement

A local authority must take reasonable steps to avoid the need for children in their area to be placed in secure accommodation. Alternatives, either day or residential, should therefore be devised.

42.7 Essential criteria for placement:

(a) the child has a history of absconding and is likely to abscond from any other description of accommodation and if s/he absconds s/he is likely to suffer significant harm; or

(b) if s/he is kept in any other description of accommodation s/he is likely to injure her/himself or other persons.

Children who satisfy the criteria in (a) and are provided with accommodation by a health authority etc. are children to whom *s 25* applies, as are children who satisfy criterion (b) and are accommodated in a residential care home etc. [*reg 7 SI 1991 No 1505*]. Until further regulations are made however only local authorities may apply to place a child in secure accommodation.

42.8 DETAINED AND REMANDED CHILDREN

Where a child is detained under *s 38(6)* of the *Police and Criminal Evidence Act 1984* (juvenile arrest) or remanded having been charged or convicted of:

(a) an offence punishable in the case of an over 21 year old with 14 years or more imprisonment; or

(b) an offence of violence having been previously convicted of an offence of violence,

the criteria for placement in secure accommodation are 'that it appears that any accommodation other than secure is inappropriate because the child is likely to abscond from such other accommodation or the child is likely to injure himself or other people if kept in any other such accommodation' [*reg 7 SI 1991 No 1505*].

42.9 Detention in secure accommodation without court authority

A child may be placed in secure accommodation for up to an aggregate of 72 hours (whether or not consecutive) in any period of 28 days. In calculating that period *reg 10* makes provision for Sundays and/or other holidays. Where a child has been detained under court authority and subsequently is placed without court authority, any period in secure accommodation before the authority was given is to be disregarded in calculating the 72 hours [*reg 10*].

42.10 Detention with court authority

A court order does not require the authority to place or keep a child in secure accommodation. The court order is merely authority to keep or place a child if the local authority so chooses (but see WARDSHIP (45) below).

The maximum initial period of any authorisation is three months. Further periods of up to six months at a time may subsequently be authorised.

For children remanded, the maximum is the period of remand or 28 days whichever is the shorter.

42.11 Secure Accommodation

42.11 PROCEDURE

Application forms are prescribed by rules of court which also prescribe who shall be made respondents to the application which will always include all those with parental responsibility for the child. If the child is already in secure accommodation in a community home, notice of intention to apply for an order must be given to parents, non-parents with parental responsibility, the independent visitor if one has been appointed and any other person the authority consider should be informed [reg 14 SI 1991 No 1505]. The application must be made by or on behalf of the local authority looking after the child [reg 8 SI 1991 No 1505] (or, when further regulations are made, other statutory bodies, the voluntary organisation or person carrying on the residential home).

The child must be legally represented unless, having been told of her/his right to apply for legal aid and having the opportunity to do so, has refused or failed to apply [CA s 25(6)].

If the court is satisfied that the relevant grounds have been made out an order authorising secure accommodation must be made. On adjournment of a hearing an interim order may be made.

42.12 REVIEW OF PLACEMENT [SI 1991 No 1505 Regs 15 and 16]

A panel of at least three, including one person independent of the local authority looking after the child, has to be established to review individual cases within one month of placement in care and then at three-monthly intervals. The panel needs to determine whether the criteria for placement continue to apply and, even so, that secure accommodation is still necessary and whether any other form of accommodation would be appropriate. The panel must ascertain the wishes and feelings of the child, any parent and other person having parental responsibility, the independent visitor, if appointed, and any other person who has had the care of the child whose views the panel consider should be taken into account and the authority managing the accommodation if not the one looking after the child.

The review requirements appear to apply only to children looked after by local authorities. When further regulations are made allowing health authorities, for example, to apply for secure accommodation orders, this may be changed.

Those persons mentioned above must also be informed of the outcome of the review and the panels reasons.

The regulations do not require written notice of intention to apply for a review or of its outcome, simply that the relevant persons be informed. It would be more in keeping with other provisions under the Act to give written notification.

43 Self-incrimination

43.1 References

Children Act 1989, s 98

43.2 Any person giving evidence in proceedings for an order under *Parts IV* and *V* of the 1989 Act cannot be excused from giving evidence and answering questions on the grounds of self-incrimination or incrimination of her/his spouse.

43.3 But a statement so made or evidence given under this provision is inadmissible in evidence against the persons making it or her/his spouse in any proceedings for an offence other than perjury.

44 Support for Families and Children

44.1 References

Children Act 1989, Part III and *Sch 2*

44.2 INTRODUCTION

This section deals with the local authority's duties to safeguard the welfare of children in need or being looked after by them, to provide services, and the range of services to be provided. Registration and inspection of day care services is dealt with in 33, foster placement in 23, reviews in 38, complaints and representations in 10, accommodation in 44.5 and charges in 4.

44.3 THE GENERAL DUTY [section 17]

The Act makes it

> 'the general duty of every local authority (in addition to the other duties imposed on them by this Part) to safeguard and promote the welfare of children within their area who are in need and so far as is consistent with that duty to promote the upbringing of such children by their families by providing a range and level of services appropriate to those children's needs'.

The phrase 'general duty' has some significance. Previous legislation made it a duty to provide such advice, guidance and assistance as may promote the welfare of children by diminishing the need to receive children into or keep them in care. Any provisions made in accordance with that duty could include provision for assistance in kind or in cash.

In *Attorney General ex rel Tilley v LB Wandsworth [1981] 1 All ER* it was held that the local authority could not fetter its discretion (by blanket denial of assistance to children of families declared to be intentionally homeless) but must consider the case of each individual child. The *Children Act* in effect overrules that case by imposing a general duty ('general' is defined in the Shorter Oxford Dictionary as 'true in most cases, but not without exceptions'; (opposite to universal)). The duty is perhaps to safeguard in most if not all cases of children in need and therefore to take decisions about provision which generally may be beneficial as opposed to examining every case where there is a family with children who may be in need.

The discretion to give assistance in kind or in exceptional cases, in cash, is no longer however directly linked to diminishing the need to seek a care order or provide accommodation. In practice preventative work with children and families may now include cash and other assistance long before accommodation is requested.

44.4 PROVISION OF SERVICES

Children in need and their families (if done with a view to safeguarding etc. the child), may be provided with services. 'Child in need' is defined as follows:

(*a*) s/he is unlikely to achieve or maintain, or have the opportunity of

Support for Families and Children 44.5

achieving or maintaining, a reasonable standard of health or development without the provision of services;

(b) her/his health or development is likely to be significantly impaired or further impaired without the provision for her/him of such services; or

(c) s/he is disabled.

'Family' in relation to the child in need includes any person with parental responsibility and any other person with whom s/he has been living.

The definition of disability takes the form of that in the *National Assistance Act 1948* (which it was argued was convenient for the transition from child to adult) although in the opinion of many the definition is archaic and ill-suited to the community care provisions of the *National Health Service and Community Care Act 1990*. Development means physical, intellectual, emotional, social or behavioural development and health means physical or mental health.

Authorities are bound to identify the extent to which there are children in need in their area and publish information about support services they provide and, where appropriate, those provided by others. They are to take reasonably practicable steps to see that those who might benefit from the services receive the information relevant to them. This will involve publicity in a form which can be understood by potential recipients i.e. translation, audio cassettes etc. A register of disabled children must also be kept, and services for disabled children must be designed to minimise the effect of disabilities and give them an opportunity to live as normal a life as possible.

Assessment of needs under the Act may be undertaken at the same time as any other assessment.

All these duties are in respect of all children in need (including therefore disabled children). Furthermore, in respect of any child there is a duty to prevent children suffering ill treatment, or neglect, to reduce the need to take court action, to avoid the need for the use of secure accommodation and to encourage children not to commit crime. The implementation of these duties will clearly allow for the widest range of preventative services being made available if resources permit.

In relation to day care and fostering services, arrangements made by local authorities must take account of the different racial groups in the area (similar provision is made for other children being looked after by local authorities).

Schedule 2 of *CA 89* deals specifically with children thought to be likely to suffer harm moving to another area; the receiving authority must be notified of the address (if possible) and the harm the child is thought likely to suffer.

44.5 RANGE OF SERVICES

Accommodation

In order to protect a child at risk from a person living at the same address an authority may assist that person to obtain alternative accommodation if s/he wishes, in cash if need be. Repayment may be required unless the person is in receipt of income support or family credit.

Accommodation must be provided for children lost or abandoned, who have no person with parental responsibility, or whose carer is prevented from providing

44.6 Support for Families and Children

suitable accommodation or care. This duty replaces 'voluntary' reception into care. The authority does not acquire any parental responsibility unless agreement is made with the person having such for the authority to exercise it under *s 2(9)*. Consent to medical treatment, for example, would be a matter for the parent etc. in the absence of any such agreement. The authority may provide accommodation even though the parent is able to provide it her/himself if that would safeguard or promote the child's welfare, but cannot accommodate a child if any person who has parental responsibility and is willing and able to provide accommodation or arrange for it to be provided objects.

Any person with parental responsibility may remove a child at any time from accommodation provided. The authority's only remedy is care proceedings if the grounds exist. *Section 8* orders or wardships are not available to a local authority in such circumstances [*ss 9(2)(5)* and *100(2)*]. It will be important evidently to specify in placement agreements, arrangements for the return of the child, although they cannot be enforced other than by establishing grounds for a care order.

The provisions for a parent etc. to remove a child or object to accommodation being provided do not apply where a residence order or High Court order is in force giving care of the child to other persons, if they agree to the child being accommodated. Nor do they apply where a child of 16 or over agrees to being accommodated.

Accommodation must also be provided for children removed under *Part V* of the Act and for remanded and detained children [*s 21*].

The local authority's duty in relation to children accommodated or in care (looked after) is dealt with in 44.3.

A wide range of provision i.e. advice, guidance and counselling, home help, occupational, social, cultural or recreational activities, holidays, assistance with travel to take up services, may be made for children living with their families. The level of service is determined by what the authority consider appropriate [*Sch 2 para 8*]. Similarly family centres are to be provided for the child, parents and others where they may attend for advice, activities etc. or be accommodated while receiving advice. If a child in need is not living with her/his family and is not offered accommodation the authority must take reasonably practicable steps to enable the child to live with her/his family or promote contact.

The duty to provide services and the range and level of services to be provided gives abundant enabling powers for preventative work with families, and their use or non-use may be critical when care proceedings are considered as courts may be reluctant to order compulsory care in such circumstances.

44.6 Children being looked after

When a child is accommodated or in care, contact with family and others must be promoted and in doing so travelling and subsistence expenses may be made to facilitate visiting if the visit would otherwise cause undue financial hardship.

The local authority may also guarantee deeds of apprenticeship or articles of clerkship for such children or those qualifying for after care (see below). The authority's services can also extend to arranging or assisting (with the approval of the court for a child in care) the child to live outside England and Wales. A child in care must give her/his consent if of sufficient understanding and the consents of other persons are also required. If the child is not in care her/his consent is not required.

44.7 After Care

The local authority have a duty to prepare a child for 'after care'. This is a new duty imposed by the *Children Act 1989*. See DOH guidance Vol 3 Ch 9 [*CA s 24*].

Any child who was looked after while over 16 and who is under 21 is a person qualifying for advice or assistance. Children not looked after but privately fostered between those ages (only a disabled child can be privately fostered after 16) or accommodated by a voluntary organisation or in a registered children's home or for a consecutive period of three months by a health education authority, or in any residential care, nursing home or mental nursing home, also qualify.

Qualifying persons who request help may be given advice and assistance. Assistance may be in kind or, in exceptional circumstances, in cash. Repayment may be demanded from those not in receipt of income support or family credit.

If the qualifying person was being looked after by a local authority, they may meet expenses incurred in living near where s/he is employed or seeking employment or receiving education or training. A grant may also be made towards education or training expenses. Any of these outlays cannot be recovered. If the education or training course of the qualifying person continued beyond 21 years of age contributions may still be made.

The responsibility for advice and assistance lies with the authority who know that there is within their area a person qualifying for advice and assistance and not necessarily therefore the authority who has looked after that person.

An authority that has advised or befriended a qualifying person must notify the authority where s/he is living or proposes to live. Voluntary organisations, residential care homes etc. and health and education authorities who have provided accommodation after a child has reached 16 must notify the local authority where the child proposes to live on leaving that accommodation. These notifications are important as an indication to the authority that the qualifying person is in their area, although it would be difficult to argue that where such a person requested help, the local authority did not know s/he was within their area.

45 Wardship

45.1 References

Children Act 1989, ss 9(1), 91(4) and 100
Guardianship of Minors Act 1973, s 2 (repealed)
Matrimonial Causes Act 1973, s 42 (repealed)
Adoption Act 1976, s 26 (repealed)
Domestic Proceedings and Magistrates' Courts Act 1978, ss 9 and 10 (repealed)
Family Law Reform Act 1969, s 7(2)
Child Care Act 1980, Part III (repealed)

45.2 INTRODUCTION

The discussion here of wardship is limited to the changes brought about by the 1989 Act which affect committal of a child to local authority care. As will be seen, the use of wardship by local authorities is now very much restricted. Wardship proceedings can still be brought by individuals who want the court to resolve private disputes. However the wide powers available to courts through the use of *s 8* orders (see SECTION 8 ORDERS (41)) and the ability of others apart from parents to apply to the court for orders concerning children means that the use of wardship in private disputes is likely to be greatly reduced. Changes affecting orders existing and proceedings pending before the Act came into force are dealt with in *Sch 14* and the *Children Act 1989 (Commencement No 2 – Amendment and Transitional Provisions) Order 1991 (SI 1991 No 1990)*.

45.3 BACKGROUND

Before the 1989 Act came into force, a child could be committed to the care of a local authority by the High Court, either under its inherent jurisdiction (an historical development of the role of the Crown as 'parent' of all minors within its jurisdiction), or under *s 7(2)* of the *Family Law Reform Act 1969* (see Lowe & White 2nd Ed). Use of the inherent jurisdiction was necessary, e.g. when the potential ward was over 17 and possibly when an interim order was sought. In both cases the court's order vested care and control of the child in the local authority, subject to any directions given, and the overriding rule that no important step in the child's life could be taken without the court's consent. Care orders made under the *Family Law Reform Act 1969* also incorporated the provisions of *Part III* of the *Child Care Act 1980* relating to the treatment of children in care.

45.4 THE EFFECT OF SECTION 100 OF THE CHILDREN ACT 1989

The Act imposes specific prohibitions on the use of the wardship jurisdiction.

(a) The statutory provision for committal to care under *s 7(2)* of the 1969 Act is abolished (as is the power to place under local authority supervision) [*s 100(1)*]; all other powers to commit to care or place under supervision in adoption and family proceedings are also repealed [*CA Schs 12, 13* and *15*].

(b) The inherent jurisdiction cannot be used to make a care order, or place a child under the supervision of a local authority, nor can it be used to require a child to be accommodated by a local authority [*s 100(2)(a)* and *(b)*].

(c) A local authority can only use the inherent jurisdiction with the leave of the court. That can only be granted if the court is satisfied that:

   (i) the desired result could not be achieved through an order under another jurisdiction (e.g. the 1989 Act) which the authority is entitled to apply for (with or without leave); and

   (ii) there is reasonable cause to believe that the child is likely to suffer significant harm if the jurisdiction is not used.

To be successful the authority must show that a specific issue or prohibited steps order, for example, would not achieve the desired result. There will be few cases left in which authorities will now be able to consider wardship, although specific issue and prohibited steps which are restricted to issues of 'parental responsibility' may be subject to judicial interpretation limiting their scope.

(d) Where a child is already subject to a care order s/he cannot be made a ward.

Previously authorities were able, and even encouraged by the courts, to supplement powers under a care order by seeking wardship. The restriction applies to any applicant local authority or any other person [*s 100(2)(c)*].

(e) The making of a care order with respect to a child who is a ward brings that wardship to an end [*s 91(4)*].

(f) The inherent jurisdiction cannot be used to enable an authority 'to determine any question which has arisen, or may arise in connection with any aspect of parental responsibility for a child'. In effect the court cannot be asked to give more responsibility than an authority may already have acquired [*s 100(2)(d)*].

This together with *ss 20(8)* and *100(2)(a)* and *(b)* which prevent any objection to a child being removed by a parent from a voluntary placement in local authority accommodation, is another expression of the rule that the only way in which an authority can acquire parental responsibility is by a care order, (or by agreements, or under *s 2(9)*, or by an emergency protection order).

In effect there is only one route into compulsory care – the care order – all other powers having been abolished, and only one test – the threshold criteria – to establish the grounds (see CARE AND SUPERVISION ORDERS (3)).

Index

A

Abduction
offences of 20.37
recovery order
— application for 20.40
— power to make 20.39
statutory provisions 20.38
Absentees
arrest 1.2
compelling, persuading, inviting or assisting, offence of 1.3
legislation 1.1
recovery of 1.4
Access
contact, replaced by 13.2
Adoption
decisions, participation in 11.10
parental responsibility
— acquisition of 28.14
— agreement by person with 28.9
residence order in proceedings 22.4
Assessment
refusal to submit to 5.9

B

Burial of child
arrangements for 17.7

C

Care order
application for 3.3
child accommodated by local authority 13.4
consultation, specific provision for 11.28
court
— child's attendance at 7.2
— powers of 3.4
criminal
— continuation of 3.7
— making 3.7
cross border transfers. *See* Cross border transfers
delay, procedures to avoid 18.4
grounds for making 3.2
interim 3.6
jurisdiction 3.5
married child not subject to 5.4
residence order discharging 19.5
section 8 order, discharging 19.4
statutory references 3.1
wishes, views and feelings of child, having regard to 5.16
Channel Islands
transfer of orders to and from 16.7
Child
court, attendance at 7.1-7.5
death of
— burial or cremation, arrangements for 17.7
— funeral expenses 17.8
— notification 17.3-17.6
— statutory references 17.1
definition 5.2
sufficient understanding, of
— decisions, and 5.15
— education, directions as to 5.14
— examination or assessment, refusal to submit to 5.9
— legal representation 5.13
— medical advice and treatment 5.10
— medical etc. treatment, agreement to 5.11
— section 8 order, application for 5.12
— statutory references 5.8
upbringing 5.17
wishes, views and feelings, having regard to 5.16
Child abuse
case conferences 6.4
changes in procedure 6.2
children's homes, in 12.20
consultation and participation 11.12
female circumcision as 6.6, 8.3
guidance on 6.2-6.4
inter-agency co-operation 2.6
investigations 6.6
removal from home 6.5
Child assessment order
applications 20.4
court, powers and duties of 20.8-20.10
grounds for 20.6
guardian ad litem, appointment of 20.11
introduction of 20.2
legal aid for 20.12

Index

procedure 20.7
refusal to comply 20.13
refusal to submit to 20.9
removal from home, specifying 13.8
summary of provisions 20.5
use of 20.6
Child in need
definition 5.7, 44.4
disabled child as 5.5
local authority support 44.4
Child of the family
meaning 5.6
Child protection. *See also* Emergency protection, consultation and participation in cases of 11.17-11.22
Childminder
definition 33.2
registration. *See* Day care
Children's homes
accommodation facilities 12.6
administration of 12.11-12.16
changes in law 12.2
child abuse in 12.20
clothes, purchase by children 12.12
conduct of
— nature and quality of accommodation, etc. 12.3
— statement of objectives 12.4
control and discipline 12.7-12.12
death of child, notification of 17.6
definitions 34.2
local authority visits 12.17-12.19
meals, choice of 12.11
records required 12.14, 12.15
registered
— inspection of 34.4
— definition of 34.2
— visits to 34.4
— voluntary 34.3
religious persuasions, respecting 12.10
responsible authority, for 17.2
schools, being 39.3
staff of 12.5
statutory references 12.1
voluntary
— definition 34.2
— inspection of 34.4
— registration 34.3
— visits to 34.4
Circumcision, female
child abuse, as 6.6, 8.3
investigation of 8.2
references 8.1

steps to prevent 8.4
Community homes
cessation, notice of 9.4
directions to accommodate child 9.8
instruments of management 9.5
responsibility for 9.2
secure accommodation in 42.5
statutory references 9.1
unsatisfactory, steps to stop use of 9.3
voluntary organisation, provided by 9.2
— management, equipment and maintenance of 9.6
— proposal to employ or terminate employment, notification of 9.7
Complaints and representations
action, consideration of 10.16
appeals 10.19
applications 10.2-10.4
complainant 10.6
— notification to 10.13
Complaints procedure directions 10.3
consideration of 10.10
grounds for 10.5
independent person, appointment of 10.11
inter-related procedures 10.7
local authority dealing with 10.12
Local Authority Ombudsman, via 10.22
making 10.8, 10.9
panel
— meeting 10.14
— recommendations and reasons, recording 10.15
— reference to 10.13
procedure
— explanation of 10.9
— monitoring 10.17
registered children's homes, involving 10.18
Secretary of State, default powers of 10.20
social services functions, concerning 10.21
statutory references 10.1
voluntary organisations, involving 10.18
Consultation and participation
adoption decisions, in 11.10
child abuse cases, in 11.12
child protection cases, in 11.17-11.22

Index

disabled person, on behalf of 11.11
English law, effect of decisions in 11.6
European material 11.4, 11.5
legislation 11.3
local authorities and other agencies, consultation and co-operation between 11.13-11.16
local authorities and public at large, between 11.23-11.25
requirement of 11.2
reviews, in 38.11
specific provision for 11.28

Contact
  access, replacing 13.2
  child accommodated by local authority 13.4
  consultation 13.3
  emergency protection order, and 20.21
  — directions in 13.8
  order. *See also* Section 8 orders
  — child, application by 13.6
  — definition 41.10
  — directions in 13.7
  — family proceedings, in 13.5
  — foster parents, application by 41.8
  — making 41.10
  — meaning 13.2
  — persons seeking 13.5
  — refusal, no further application after 19.6
  — restrictions on 13.6
  police protection, child in 13.8, 20.29
  promotion of 13.3
  statutory references 13.1

Contraceptive advice
  child, for 5.10

Council of Europe
  Recommendations and Resolutions 11.8

County courts
  cases started in 15.3
  classes of 15.2
  private, proceedings heard in 30.7

Court
  child's attendance at 7.1-7.5
  county courts 15.2
  family proceedings 15.2
  High Court 15.2
  proceedings, starting 15.3

reports to
— oral or in writing 36.5
— request for 36.2
— service of 36.3
— statutory references 36.1
— welfare 36.4
structure, statutory references 15.1
tiers 15.2
transfer of proceedings 15.4

Cremation of child
  arrangements for 17.7

Cross border transfers
  care orders 16.4, 16.5
  England and Wales and Northern Ireland, Channel Islands and Isle of Man, between 16.7
  regulations 16.2
  Scotland, to and from 16.3
  statutory references 16.1
  supervision orders 16.6

D

Day care
  definitions 33.2
  equipment 33.7
  inspection 33.10
  registration
  — appeals 33.11
  — application for 33.6
  — cancellation of 33.9
  — disqualified persons 33.7
  — domestic premises 33.8
  — emergency action 33.9
  — exemption from requirement 33.4
  — failure, consequences of 33.5
  — non-domestic premises 33.8
  — persons requiring 33.3
  — refusal of, 33.7
  — requirements 33.8
  review of services 11.20, 11.21
  statutory references 33.1

Death
  child, of
  — burial or cremation, arrangements for 17.7
  — funeral expenses 17.8
  — notification 17.3-17.6
  — statutory references 17.1

Delay
  jurisdiction and procedure 18.6
  procedures to avoid
  — care order 18.4

Index

— court rules 18.5
— family proceedings 18.3
— generally 18.2
— supervision order 18.4
statutory references 18.1
Dental treatment
consent of child to 5.11
Disabled children
children in need, as 5.5
local authority support 44.4
meaning 5.5
Disabled person
decisions, participation in 11.11
Divorce
children
— arrangements for 22.7
— parents attending court, whether 22.8
— position of 22.6
proceedings for 22.5

E

Education
minimum standards of 28.5
supervision orders 3.8-3.10
Emergency protection
applications 20.4
general principles 20.4
order
— appeals 20.24
— applications 20.4
— Cleveland Inquiry guidelines 20.19
— contact, and 20.21
directions on 13.8
— court, powers and duties of 20.22
— direction to disclose 20.31
— discharge of 20.23
— discovery and entry 20.30
— effect of 20.18
— entry and search 20.32
— evidence 20.17
— grounds for 20.6, 20.16
— introduction of 20.2
— obstruction 20.34
— offences 20.25
— parental responsibility, acquisition of 28.14
— police, application by 20.28
— procedure 20.15
— return of child 20.20
— summary of provisions 20.5
— use of 20.14

— warrant, execution of 20.33
police protection. *See* Police protection
prior investigation 20.3
short-term 20.2
statutory references 20.1
European Convention on Human Rights
rights in 11.4
European Convention on the Adoption of Children
enquiries required by 11.7
European Social Charter
enforcement of 11.9
Examination
refusal to submit to 5.9

F

Family assistance orders
making 21.2
Family proceedings
adoption proceedings 22.4
definition 22.3
private, heard in 30.6, 30.7
section 8 order, power to make 22.2
starting 15.3
transfer of 15.4
Family proceedings court
cases started in 15.3
jurisdiction 15.2
Family support services
consultation and participation in 11.22, 11.23
Financial support
children, of 22.9
Foster parents
approval of
— general or specific 23.8
— individual 23.7
— local authority 23.5
— referees 23.6
— refusal, written notice of 23.9
— reviews 23.10, 23.11
— statutory provisions 23.4
— termination of 23.10, 23.11
different racial groups, from 32.3
residence or contact 8 orders, application for 41.8
Fostering
agreements 23.12, 23.13
children placed by voluntary organisations 23.26

Index

— visits to 23.30-23.33
limit on number of children 23.34, 23.35
— exemptions 23.36-23.39
local authority service 23.2-23.4
more than three children, of 34.2
placements
— agreement 23.17
— emergency 23.24
— immediate 23.25
— other authorities, approved by 23.16
— outside England and Wales 23.23
— religious persuasion, parents of same 23.15
— removal of child 23.21
— short-term 23.22
— suitable, where 23.14
— supervision of 23.18, 23.19
— termination of 23.20
— voluntary organisations, by 23.26
private
— advertising 31.13
— appeals 31.10
— background to 31.2
— local authority powers 31.6
— notices 31.4, 31.5
— offences 31.14
— privately fostered child, definition 31.3
— prohibition of 31.7, 31.10
— requirements, imposition of 31.8, 31.10
— schools, children in during holidays 31.11
— statutory references 31.1
— termination of placement 31.12
— welfare, safeguard of 31.6, 31.9
records 23.27-23.29
statutory references 23.1

G

Guardians
appointment
— court, by 24.5
— effect of 24.2
— private 24.4
parental responsibility, acquisition of 28.14
statutory references 24.1
Guardians ad litem
appointment 25.2
— termination of 25.9
child assessment order, where considered 20.11
independence of 25.5
panels 25.6-25.8
powers and duties of 25.4
specific duties 25.4
specified proceedings, for 25.2, 25.3
statutory references 25.1

H

Health information
access to 2.2
High Court
applications made in 15.3
Family Division 15.2
private, proceedings heard in 30.7

I

Illegitimacy
legal disabilities, disappearance of 5.3
Independent visitor
appointment
— child refusing 5.12
— consultation as to 26.4
— duty of 26.3
— termination of 26.6
duties of 26.5
statutory references 26.1, 26.2
Inquiry
Secretary of State holding 40.4
Isle of Man
transfer of orders to and from 16.7

J

Judicial separation. *See* Divorce

L

Legal aid
Children Act proceedings, in 20.12
civil proceedings, in 27.2
criminal proceedings, in 27.3
statutory references 27.1
Local authorities
accommodation, remand to. *See* Remands
charge for services
— individual liability 4.2-4.4
— inter-authority 4.5-4.7
— legislation 4.1
— means testing 4.4

Index

— ordinary residence, determining 4.7
— reasonable 4.3
— types of 4.2
child accommodated by
— after care 44.7
— agreement with parents etc. 11.26
— contact with 13.4
— death of 17.4
— remand, after 35.2
— support for families 44.6
— voluntary arrangement, as 11.27
child looked after by, maintenance of
— agreement on contribution 14.4, 14.5
— contribution orders 14.6, 14.7
— enforcement 14.8, 14.9
— liability to contribute 14.2
— persons liable 14.3
— statutory references 14.1
children's homes, visiting 12.17-12.19, 34.4
community homes. See Community homes
complaint, dealing with 10.12
consultation, specific provision for 11.28
female circumcision, investigation of 8.2
fostering service 23.2-23.4
other agencies, consultation and co-operation between 11.13-11.16
parental responsibility, acquisition of 28.14
public at large, consultation and participation 11.23-11.25
respite care
— provision of 37.2, 37.3
— reviews 38.8
— statutory references 37.1
reviews by 38.5
support for families and children
— accommodation, provision of 44.5
— after care 44.7
— child in need, definition 44.4
— children being looked after 44.6
— duties as to 44.2, 44.3
— range of services 44.5-44.7
— services, provision of 44.4
— statutory references 44.1

Local education authority
assistance, requesting 11.15, 11.16
education supervision order, application for 22.13

M

Maintenance order
duration of 19.2
Marriage
minor, of, consent to 28.11
Medical treatment
consent to 28.8
— child, of 5.11

N

Northern Ireland
transfer of orders to and from 16.7
Nullity. See Divorce

O

Orders
duration of
— general rule 19.2
— section 8 orders 19.3-19.6
— statutory references 19.1
no further application, for 19.7, 19.8

P

Parental responsibility
acquisition of 28.14
adoption, agreement to 28.9
agreement 28.14
agreement on arrangements for child 28.4
day to day decisions, making 28.4
definition 28.2
determining 5.3
education, minimum standards of 28.5
effect of 28.3
father of illegitimate child, acquisition by 28.14
loss of 28.12
marriage, consent to 28.11
married parents, of 28.13
medical treatment, consent to 28.8
order 28.14
passport, consent to obtaining 28.10
religious upbringing, as to 28.7
sharing 28.12
Passport
consent to obtaining 28.10

Index

Personal information, access to
  Data Protection Registrar, guideline of 2.4
  entitlement to 2.2
  guidance on 2.5
  legislation 2.1
  participation of children in decisions, relating to 2.3
Police protection
  contact with child 20.29
  designated police officer 20.28
  direction to disclose 20.31
  discovery and entry 20.30
  duration of 20.26
  entry and search 20.32
  notice of 20.27
  obstruction 20.34
  Police and Criminal Evidence Act, provisions of 20.35
  refuges 20.41
  summary of provisions 20.5
  warrant, execution of 20.33
Privacy
  absence of party, proceedings in 30.5
  child, identification of 30.2
  family proceedings, of 30.6, 30.7
  reporting restrictions 30.2-30.4
  statutory references 30.1
Proceedings
  absence of party, in 30.5
  family. *See* Family proceedings
  parties to
  — Children Act, under 29.2
  section 8 orders, for 29.3, 29.4
  statutory references 29.1
Prohibited steps order. *See also* Section 8 orders
  definition 41.11
  making 41.11

R

Race
  adequate care, providing 32.5
  decisions, consideration when making 32.4
  foster parents from different racial groups 32.3
  statutory references 32.1
  UN Convention of Rights of the Child 32.6
Recovery
  local authority care, children taken from 1.4

Refuges
  provision of 20.41
Registered children's homes
  complaints concerning 10.18
Religious upbringing
  adequate care, providing 32.5
  decisions, consideration when making 32.4
  determining 28.7
  importance of 32.2
  statutory references 32.1
  UN Convention of Rights of the Child 32.6
Remands
  local authority accommodation to 35.2
  named person, no requirement to live with 35.4
  placement, as 35.3
  secure accommodation 42.8
  statutory references 35.1
Residence order. *See also* Section 8 orders
  adoption proceedings, in 22.4
  care order, discharging 19.5
  foster parents, application by 41.8
  making 41.9
  meaning 41.9
  parental responsibility, acquisition of 28.14
Respite care
  provision of 37.2, 37.3
  reviews 38.8
  statutory references 37.1
Reviews
  application of provisions 38.4
  body holding 38.5
  co-ordination 38.13
  consultation 38.10
  content of 38.15
  meeting being 38.6
  participation 38.11
  procedure 38.9
  requirements, summary of 38.3-38.5
  result and decisions, notifying 38.12
  short term placements, for 38.8
  statutory references 38.1
  system of 38.2
  timing 38.7
  written report 38.14

S

Schools

148

Index

children's homes, being 39.3
independent 39.2
non-maintained special 39.3
residential care homes, being, 39.3
safeguarding welfare, child's 39.2
statutory references 39.1
Scotland
  transfer of orders to and from 16.3
Search warrants
  issue of 20.36
  reasonable force, use of 20.33
Secretary of State, powers of
  background 40.2
  default 40.2
  financial support, giving 40.5
  inquiries, ordering 40.4
  inspection 40.3
  research and returns of information 40.6
  statutory references 40.1
Section 8 orders. *See also* Residence order, etc.
  application for 41.6
  — child, by 5.12, 29.4
  — leave, for 41.7
  — local authority foster parents, restrictions on 41.8
  application to make, vary or discharge 41.2
  care order discharging 19.4
  child as party to proceedings 29.3, 29.4
  delay, procedures to avoid 18.3
  directions and conditions 41.4
  duration of 19.3
  family proceedings, in 22.2
  interim 41.3
  length of 41.5
  types of 41.2
  welfare as paramount consideration 41.2
  wishes, views and feelings of child, having regard to 5.16
Secure accommodation
  child to whom provisions applied 42.3
  community home, use of 42.5
  definitions 42.2
  detained or remanded children, for 42.8
  detention with court authority 42.10
  detention without court authority 42.9
  placement
    — avoiding 42.6
    — essential criteria 42.7
    — review of 42.12
  procedure 42.11
  special cases 42.4
  statutory references 42.1
Self-incrimination
  exclusion of 43.2, 43.3
  statutory references 43.1
Solicitor
  child, court appointing to represent 5.13
Specific issue order. *See also* Section 8 orders
  definition 41.11
  making 41.11
Supervision order
  application for 3.3
  court
    — child's attendance at 7.2
    — powers of 3.4
  cross border transfers. See Cross border transfers
  delay, procedures to avoid 18.4
  education
    — child in care, not made for 22.15
    — directions to child 5.14
    — duration of 22.17
    — effect of 22.16
    — failure to comply 22.18
    — local education authority, application by 22.13
    — making 22.12
    — properly educated, definition of 22.14
  grounds for making 3.2
  interim 3.6
  jurisdiction 3.5
  married child not subject to 5.4
  statutory references 3.1
  wishes, views and feelings of child, having regard to 5.16
Surgical treatment
  consent of child to 5.11

U

United Nations
  Convention on Rights of the Child 32.6

V

Voluntary organisations
  community home provided by 9.2

Index

— management, equipment and maintenance of 9.6
— proposal to employ or terminate employment, notification of 9.7
complaints concerning 10.18
fostering placements by 23.26
— visits to children 23.30-23.33

W

Wardship
background 45.3
changes in 45.2
prohibitions on use of jurisdiction 45.4
statutory references 45.1